"YESU MASIKI JAY"

"YESU MASIKI JAY"

["Victory to Jesus the Messiah"]

by

Gideon B. and Audrey Williamson

A Firsthand Survey of Nazarene Missionary Progress
In India

BEACON HILL PRESS
Kansas City, Missouri

First Printing, 1952

Printed in the United States of America

CONTENTS

FOREWORD

This book has grown out of a recent visit to our Nazarene mission field in Berar, Central Provinces, India. We have collaborated in setting forth the impressions and the information gained in four weeks of contact with our missionaries, national Christians, and the yet untouched thousands of this needy land. At the request of the Commission on Foreign Missionary Study Literature these facts have been published. Any royalties accruing from the sale of this book are to be returned to the country it describes, there to assist in purchasing a permanent location for the annual Indian district camp meeting, a memorial to the late General Superintendent J. B. Chapman.

THE AUTHORS

"Yesu Masiki Jay"

The Indian people have a distinctive shout of victory.

"Mahatma Gandhiki Jay!" rang from millions of loyal throats in tribute to the little man who so profoundly influenced Indian affairs.

Now, *"Nehruki Jay!"* is heard in every political gathering, a symbolic recognition of India's newly gained independence.

Our Christian groups have adopted the slogan. They shout, *"Yesu Masiki Jay!"* "Victory to Jesus, the Messiah!" It is a moving thing to hear these noble bands, with great fervor and zeal, voice this conviction and this prophecy.

The victory of Jesus Christ is the purpose of our mission. It is the hope of India. Every problem which confronts this land—economic, social, industrial, political—can be solved when He is Conqueror.

It is with the earnest desire that this book may help to speed His victory that it is presented. The progress of the Nazarene mission in India has been the victory of Jesus, the Messiah. And for Him we claim future conquests. We cry with our Indian Christians,

"Yesu Masiki Jay!"

The India of Today

No one would profess to acquire a comprehensive knowledge of India in a visit of one month. We did, however, have opportunity to gain some valuable impressions of life as it is in the India of today. We arrived in Bombay on January 26, which was the first anniversary of the signing of the constitution for the Republic, and a national holiday. This was a hindrance to us in taking care of some of the necessary business of our trip. But it did give us a chance to see something of Indian life that we might otherwise have missed. Having arrived early in the morning, we had some time to look around. As we rode along Marine Drive, we saw tens of thousands of people milling around on the beach or listening in a desultory fashion to something being transmitted to them through a public address system. In a city park again we saw the throngs. We drove by a few homes of fabulous wealth. There were imposing public buildings, modern means of transportation, and impressive institutions of learning which told us that Bombay was a great and growing city. But before we entrained for Malkapur we saw people lying on the streets, and we were informed that they would spend the night there because they had nowhere else to go. Women could be seen cooking on a fire of sticks or washing clothes on the pavement. Beggars were everywhere.

As for seeing India's sights of natural wonders or great historic significance, we did not have the time to spend that way. When he knew we were coming, Rev. L. C. Fritzlan wrote to suggest that it would require at least thirty-five days to do the work that was needed in the

Council Meeting, Assembly, and camp meeting and to touch the main points of interest on the district, and allow some time for sight-seeing. But our schedule was already made up, and there was no way to lengthen our stay. Therefore we wrote to Brother Fritzlan to omit trips to such places as Agra to see the Taj Mahal, Kashmir, Delhi, and the Himalayan Mountains. We felt our trip to India was in the interests of our mission. We made the most of our twenty-seven days to fulfill that purpose. Except for the time necessarily spent in Bombay or en route to and from our district, we were not away from our territory but for a few hours, and then only because we must be to reach one of the more remote areas of our field. The things most visitors to India go to see we passed by, but what others might call a sacrifice only proved to be a blessing to us, for we saw Indian village life again and again, and that is India, for 85 per cent of her people live in the villages.

We were in Pusad, one of the larger villages of our district, on bazaar day. There was also a cattle show in progress. Again the crowd was enormous. As they moved about, it almost seemed the surface of the earth was in motion. In other villages on bazaar days the impression was the same. This was a vivid reminder of India's vast population. In India alone there are over 300,000,000 people, with another 100,000,-000 in Pakistan. This means that 255,000,000 people live packed together in the mud houses of the 650,000 villages. None of them live on their farms, as the American people do. They are crowded into those dusty, vermin-infested, disease-ridden villages. Sanitation and hygiene are unknown. As usual, filth, disease, immorality, and illiteracy are inseparable. Some organized efforts are now being promoted by the government to reduce the illiteracy. It was 90 per cent, but now it is thought that it may be no more than 85 to 87 per cent.

A review of the long history of India would be a most interesting study. There have been periods of prosperity and glory. To those times the people of the present refer with pride. India has produced philosophers and authors of distinction. She has a literature and a culture which commands respect. While her wealth has been dissipated by misuse, she still has resources that could be developed in building a great nation.

A history of India is a history of Hinduism for many centuries. This ancient, complex, polytheistic religion has dominated the thinking of the masses and warped their lives. No other religion has been able to challenge seriously the domination of Hinduism. India produced Buddha. For a time his followers multiplied rapidly. His teachings were, in fact, in the nature of a reform within Hinduism. Eventually great persecution arose against the Buddhists, and now less than 1 per cent of the population of India are followers of Buddha. The strongholds of Buddhism are in other Asiatic countries. In India, for the most part Buddhism has been absorbed in Hinduism. One of the characteristics of this great religion is that it is all-absorbing. It receives into itself the teachings of other faiths and, in its so doing, their distinctions are compromised until there are no distinguishing differences.

In the more recent centuries the Moslem religion invaded India and did offer some effective challenge to the Hindu religion. But now the partition of India has placed the majority of Mohammedans in Pakistan. This leaves only a comparatively small minority in India. Hinduism is again supreme.

The history of Christianity in India shows intermittent progress. It seems reasonably certain that the tradition that St. Thomas went as an apostle of Christ to India in the first century has foundation in fact. Even now there is a group which is designated as the "Christians of St. Thomas." It was about the middle of the sixteenth century that St. Francis Xavier reached Goa, India. In that part of India the Catholic church has a large following. It is active elsewhere also. On the ship by which we sailed from Adelaide, Australia, to Bombay, we were served in the dining room by two men who proudly informed us that they were Christians from Goa, followers of St. Francis Xavier.

The work of Protestant missions was begun in India by William Carey in the year 1793. Today there are 10,-000,000 Christians. This means that Christianity is the third largest religious group in India. If the ratio of increase of the last century can be maintained for another hundred years, Christ will have completed the conquest of India.

This gives rise to the question of whether proselyting is permissible. There are many considerations which arise in a discussion of that problem. One pertinent question is, "What has Hinduism with its 330,000,000 deities done for the millions of India?" It has left them, after many centuries, one of the most backward nations of the world. The masses are in abject poverty. Many of them are beggars. Millions never have their hunger satisfied in a lifetime. Nearly 90 per cent of the people are illiterate. They agree that woman is depraved and the cow is sacred. Monkeys, cobras, and peacocks are objects of worship. All forms of life are revered. Rats may invade a village, bringing the plague. No attempt will be made to exterminate them. The villagers will evacuate their homes until the rats leave.

Hinduism has saddled the caste system upon India. Caste is a series of social strata which classifies all men according to their occupation. Its law is inexorable. None can ever break caste. Mahatma Gandhi was opposed to the caste system. The new constitution of free India has outlawed it in theory. But a people whose minds have been so deeply grooved by centuries of custom and practice will not be changed by a constitutional denial of the existence of such a system. We talked with a high caste Brahmin, a former university professor. He expressed disapproval of any attempt to offer the depressed classes better standards of living through sanitation, hygiene, and medical care. He declared that only the free operation of the law of the survival of the fittest would take care of excessive population. He felt that the 400 per cent increase in food costs since World War II had imposed a hardship on those of his own social standing, but it did not matter for those who work hard for ten to twenty-two cents a day.

Do people who are enslaved by such a religion need a Saviour? Let all who know the Christian way of life answer for themselves.

It is not the purpose of the Christian missionary to introduce the Western way of life to the Orient. We recognize that in our own social order there is much that is unchristian. We do not profess to have achieved the ideal economic, social, and industrial system. We do believe that in the gospel of Jesus Christ the Way, the Truth, and the Life are set forth. We do believe that Christ is the Light of the World and that if men will receive Him as Saviour, follow Him as Teacher, and obey Him as Lord they will find the better life here and eternal life hereafter.

In any comparison of the religions of the world the teachings of Jesus Christ will stand alone above them all. For reasonable content, for ethical ideals, for practical results in the lives of those who follow Christ, the religion that He founded is beyond comparison.

Another question frequently asked is, "What is the Indian attitude toward communism?" India is rapidly developing a spirit of nationalism. She does not want a return to domination by any other nation. She would resist that vigorously whether it be by Britain, Russia, or America. The official attitude of the leaders of India is one that any nation would seek to maintain which had so recently achieved a long-sought independence; it is that India will face her own problems and find their solution without interference from other countries. The long domination of Oriental countries by Europeans makes them suspicious of anything that looks like an encroachment upon their right of self-government and self-determination. That the country needs economic aid to establish itself among the great nations of the world in proportion to its population, there can be no doubt. But India does not want to be looked upon as a pauper among the people of the earth. If a plan of economic assistance can be offered that will increase the productiveness of the soil, develop the natural resources and industrial possibilities, and thus lift the standard of living among the people, it will be good. This will be, in the long run, not only an investment in friendly relations but also in peace and prosperity that will benefit both those who invest and those in whom the investment is made. India will accept the help gratefully and will cooperate with it willingly. She will not be pauperized, neither will she be enslaved.

Many are puzzled by the attitude of Nehru toward Red China, but all of Asia is in a mood to resist aggression from nations of other areas of the world. Whether expressed in that language or not, they want Asia for the Asiatics. To a country that adhered to the Monroe Doctrine for a century, that attitude should not be hard to understand.

India will not willingly fall under the control of Russia, nor will she adopt the Soviet brand of communism. Communism is gaining a foothold in India, especially in the south. The depressed classes, who are in such large majority, offer a fertile seedbed for the communistic doctrines. The need of economic and social change is apparent. The people are ready to accept economic improvement regardless of the name of the system by which it is offered. Nevertheless, India is essentially a religious nation. She will not readily accept a godless philosophy.

A friendly, helpful attitude toward India on the part of the Christian democratic nations of the world, together with a great advance in the work of Christian evangelism and education, will bear fruit in a most rewarding harvest of good. It should be recognized, also, that India has a contribution to make to the peace and prosperity of the world. Let us offer her a place of equality and comradeship in the great family of nations. Let us give freely, and we shall receive many benefits for ourselves and our posterity.

British influence in India is another factor that will retard the progress of communism in the country. For many years Britain sponsored free, fair, and democratic elections. To a people so educated, the methods of a totalitarian state will not be readily accepted. Furthermore, the foundations of the present government of India were laid by the British rulers. That the present government of the country is entirely satisfactory no one would claim. But in that, India is not unlike other nations of the world, including our own great country.

It is hoped that American statesmen will seek to understand India and her leaders. We should remember that she is an Oriental country. We must not seek to westernize her. We should recognize her points of greatness and then offer to her the gospel of Christ with all its blessed by-products. In her hour of need let us give of our abundance for humanitarian reasons. We belittle ourselves and offend India when we confuse benevolence with political intrigue.

The question of India's attitude toward the Western democracies is inescapable. This, of course, includes the relation of India and Britain. Let it be said here that the stories of domination and exploitation of India by the British have been much exaggerated. That the entire history of British rule in India is praiseworthy no one would presume to declare. But that there was some advantage to India none can deny. After fifteen years' residence in India and repeated visits thereafter, Sherwood Eddy said that on the whole, together with the Philippines, he knew of no finer instance in history of the government of one people by another.

When the long struggle of India for independence reached its goal through the leadership of Gandhi, Britain withdrew in a most commendable manner. The evacuation was conducted under the leadership of the last viceroy, Lord Mountbatten. We were told on reliable authority that in Bombay during those last days the people would shout, *"Mahatma Gandhiki Jay!"* Which translated into English is, "Victory to Mahatma Gandhi!" Then the crowd would also shout, *"Mountbattenki Jay!"* or, "Victory to Mountbatten!" It is also significant that after the differences were settled the Indian government voted to accept dominion status in the British Commonwealth of Nations.

We were entertained for tea at the bungalow of the deputy commissioner of the district of Buldana. He was a man of learning and culture. He spoke excellent English. He volunteered this observation: "There was a time when Britain and America were enemies; now they are the best of friends. Likewise, not long ago India and Britain were hostile toward one another; now they are the best of friends."

This same man in an address before a great crowd of farmers extolled the accomplishments of America in changing a wilderness into the world's most productive country. He then challenged his countrymen to undertake the problems confronting India in that spirit of energy and industry which had made America successful.

The people and leaders of India are cautious, and to some extent they may be said to be suspicious. But if we of the West deal with them in candor, fairness, and righteousness they will respond, and they can become the greatest ally and friend of democracy in all Asia.

And now, what is the measure of the total impact of Christianity upon the vast population of India? That question is impossible of an adequate answer. No one man or any number of men can estimate what Christ has done for India. To say there are 10,000,000 who profess to be Christians in India does not tell the whole story by any means. There are probably as many more "secret believers" who are convinced that Christ is the only Saviour and whose lives have in some degree been changed by His teachings. To number the Christian institutions, schools, hospitals, orphanages, and churches would not be sufficient to reveal the transformations the gospel has accomplished.

The presence of Christian men in the government in far greater proportion than those representing other religions has meaning also. We met three government officials of various ranks. One was an ardent witness for Christ. Another declared he had called the Nazarene missionaries to pray for his little girl when the doctors told him she would die. He added, "I have my child with me now, well and strong, because God heard their prayers." The third said, "Christian nations seek to promote peace and justice among men."

Leaders of India such as Gandhi and Dr. Ambedkar have confessed a great debt to Jesus Christ and His teachings.

India offers many problems to be solved by her leaders. She is a challenge to the Christian world. Her handicaps are many, but she has much to inspire the devotion and sacrifice of the Christian Church. Let us seek to understand India. Let us pray for her. Let us give Christ to her more than 300,000,000 people.

Arrival

The night mail train from Bombay to Malkapur lurched to an uncertain stop. Stooping, I peered out through the window of our compartment into the gray light of coming dawn. Indian men clad in dhotis, with heads swathed in turbans and shoulders wrapped in blankets, passed by on the station platform. Coolies, in red shirts, carrying tin boxes or wooden trunks of great weight on their heads, trotted by with rhythmic pace, the litheness of their step serving to counteract somewhat the heavy pull of gravity upon their bodies. Vendors of tea, sweetmeats, and spicy food called their wares in a minor chant. Women in saris of green or blue or maroon squatted or sat with little children huddled about them, or with babies tugging at their breasts. Here and there on the stone pavement lay a huddle of dirty cloth where an old man or woman still slept, unaroused by the waking day's activity.

I turned away, my heart full of compassion. Came a loud knock at the door on the station side. It was not the first time that night, for at several stops there had been banging outside from someone hunting a place to get into the train. In India each compartment—whether first, second, or third class—is an individual unit, and can be entered only from the station platform. Except from terminal points, reservations cannot be made in advance, and it is a case of "every man for himself" and "first come, first served." The doors are bolted from within, and if one cannot gain entrance he waits for another train.

But as I turned back to the window, this time I saw the smiling face of our missionary chairman, Leslie Fritzlan, and quickly opened the door.

"Are you all right? How did you rest? Now, next stop will be Malkapur! Just let me have your bedrolls and I'll have them fixed up by the time we get there. Guess I'd better hurry back before the train starts." And he was gone.

In a short time we were piling out at Malkapur station to be greeted by Rev. and Mrs. P. L. Beals and Mrs. Fritzlan, who had brought breakfast for us. This we ate in the bare little station waiting room, where years before Dr. R. T. Williams and Dr. J. W. Goodwin had spent a long night due to an error in telegraph connections. We smiled to visualize them as they do doubt were swayed back and forth between patience and weariness, fortitude and exasperation.

We were surprised to find that the local band was out with various types of horns and a bass drum greeting us with a doleful tune, all air and no harmony. Someone deflated us a bit by telling us that they were not there to welcome us but some Indian official who had happened to arrive on the same train. But dear Brother Beals fixed it all up by slipping over to them and asking them please to oblige by playing something for the "General from America." And did they do it! They did, with gusto! They were repeating the chorus for the second time when I said, "That sounds a little like 'A Bicycle Built for Two.'" And it was, without a doubt! How pleased we were, and what could have been more appropriate!

Mr. and Mrs. Fritzlan and Samuel Bhujbal, Indian district superintendent, were off in the carryall (which it invariably does) and disappeared down the winding road in a whirl of dust. We followed in the 1950 Chevrolet, the "miracle car" of Mr. and Mrs. Beals, with Mrs. Ruby Blackman. The rolling land covered with a sparse growth of low bush stretched away to the horizon. The road was lined with mango and neem trees, which at times made a leafy arch overhead. The long briers of the acacia, from which it is said Christ's crown of thorns was composed, were also in evidence.

The oncoming traffic was the two-wheeled bullock carts, for the most part, this day, piled high with cotton, tufted at the sides or back with a sheaf of fodder for the animals. The turbaned driver, often accompanied by another man, perched on top or squatted in front of his load. If the bullocks seemed frightened by the car, he stopped them and held taut the rope reins, running through their nostrils. If they were unusually nervous, another driver held their heads until we had passed, as they are liable to wheel and turn the vehicle around or even off the road. Sometimes the cart held a load of four or five men, or perhaps women and children, protected from the sun by an arched bamboo canopy. I had known there would be bullock carts. I did not know there would be hundreds of them. Once in making this forty-two-mile journey by car from Malkapur to Chikhli, Ralph Cook said he counted the bullock carts. He passed two hundred going and the same two hundred in returning.

These men often travel in companies, especially at night, as a protection against thieves. One may meet twelve or fifteen at a stretch, the eyes of the oxen gleaming in the beam from the headlights of the car like balls of fire. Sometimes one comes on a caravan halted for the night, the animals loose from their carts, munching their feed, and the drivers sitting on their haunches around a roadside fire.

These farmers, men of the Maratha caste, laid hold of our hearts. It is to them that the Lord especially called Samuel Bhujbal one Sunday morning in Dallas, Texas, while on his recent visit to the United States. A few of these men have stepped out and boldly accepted Jesus Christ, but as a class they have been as yet untouched by the gospel appeal. They are attending our services in some places in large numbers. It would be a wonderful thing for them and for the Church of the Nazarene and for India if they could be reached by Jesus Christ and His redeeming grace.

As we passed they gazed at us with deep, impenetrable eyes, with interest, yet without emotion. There was no salaam or nod of greeting, but a fixed, intelligent, inscrutable gaze. They did not smile, they did not frown, they only looked. It was so with those we passed walking on the road, an occasional man or group of women with bundles of firewood or with vessels on their heads. They did not recognize us, they did not ignore us. With dignity and with poise they accepted us.

Occasionally off a bit from the road would appear a low mound of gray. As we came closer, an Indian village would be discernible. Here is where Indian life lives and moves. In India proper there are six hundred and fifty thousand of these villages, ranging in population from two hundred to two thousand, and in some instances ten or fifteen thousand. Villages were formerly surrounded by mud walls for protection. In Berar Province these have wasted away. Here and there a portion still stands. The homes, especially of the smaller villages, are all of mud walls with thatched or corrugated iron roofs. The houses face on the crooked, narrow streets where men and women walk, naked children play, and cows, chickens, and goats wander. There is no color except in the dress of the women or the red and yellow turbans of the men—no gaily painted houses, no bright and fragrant flower beds. There is no shade except in the shadow of a wall or an occasional tree. There is no respite from the dust and filth except at the well, where women come with brass and earthen pots to chat a bit and carry home water, unpurified and disease-ridden, yet still so necessary and so precious.

As we approached Buldana our hearts beat more quickly. Here was our first Nazarene mission station. Here Rev. and Mrs. L. S. Tracy had lived and labored. Here May McKay and little Buddy were laid to rest fifteen years ago.

At the mission bungalow we stopped a moment to be greeted by the Weldon Franklin and Clarence Carter families, who received us with warm handclasps and a hearty welcome. We were soon off for Chikhli, where the Bealses and the Fritzlans and Mrs. Blackman live and where the coeducational school is located. This town of ten thousand is the county seat, and its government buildings of painted stone with tiled roofs are quite impressive. The two-story home of a well-to-do merchant and a Hindu shrine caught our attention as we entered the town.

But then Brother Beals turned, in spite of his wife's remonstrance, to take us through the old section of the village. His purpose was to show us the native hut where Dr. Julia Gibson and Mrs. Ella Perry had lived. We made our way over the narrow, rocky, twisted street, the car horn blowing constantly to prevent hitting man or beast. In the doorways old women squatted, teeth and eyesight all but gone. Men sat before their dwellings on their haunches, clasping their knees, while they spat the red betel juice on walls and earthen floors. Little children, naked except for bracelets and anklets and rings in ears or nose, perched astride the hips of older brothers or sisters, who stared at us as we passed. These older ones had usually a single garment, very dirty and full of holes. The hair of the little girls, gray with dust or ashes, was in a frowzy tumble. One old man lay at the edge of the road, apparently asleep, where he had crawled out of his hut to warm his failing limbs in the sun. Mothers sat with naked babies lying in their laps, the eyes of some almost closed with infection, and upon the bodies of others open sores smeared with tar. Smoke billowed from the doors of some houses, for it was nearing the time for the preparation of the noon meal. A cow ambled across the road and we stopped until she had passed. Everywhere eyes followed us—dark, staring eyes; faces empty, resigned, from childhood to old age bound by a system of philosophy from which there was no respite or recourse. They were born to be thus; thus they would ever be. Occasionally there was a shop or a place where food was sold. Dust, smells, excrement, flies, and filth— this was the picture.

With heavy heart I sat back as we left the town and climbed the hill to the Nazarene mission station. I closed my eyes. "Dear God," I prayed, "isn't there anything we can do about it?"

And then the car was stopping at the mission compound. On either side of the drive poles had been driven into the ground, and from them festoons of gay little paper flags fluttered bravely in the breeze. Over the gateway was a welcome sign, and lining the drive clear to the mission house stood in double row our Nazarene Christians from the coeducational school. There was the headmaster, John Meshramker, and his wife Anandabai; the pastor, Brother Salve, and his wife, who assists at the dispensary. There were the teachers and the matron and the boys' monitor, and the boys and girls themselves ranging in age from eight to sixteen years. The saris of the girls were freshly laundered and they looked like a flower garden—pink, blue, yellow, violet, and green. The boys' shirts and shorts were spotless. All were clothed and in their right minds. Their hair was combed and parted, and they looked as though they had been anointed with fresh oil (as no doubt they had been).

Introductions to the teachers came first, and we were garlanded by two tiny girls, while words of welcome were sung and spoken. Then, smiling through a blur of tears, we walked between the waiting lines where every hand was raised in salute and "Salaam, salaam" met us on either side. Beautiful brown faces were all alight, smiling, teeth gleaming, and eyes once dark and blank now glowing with delight, with hope, and with purpose.

It was a thrilling moment! As I passed down that line I felt as Queen Elizabeth must have felt when she went with her husband to view the empire. I, too, represented the King, and our King is worthy of all praise! It was the most overwhelming testimony that I have ever witnessed to the power of the gospel of Jesus Christ to transform lives and to lift men. I marveled at His grace. Here on the one hand was humanity, dirty, disease-ridden, fixed, and hopeless. On the other hand was the same humanity, touched by the gospel, clean, happy, radiant, transformed. Glory to His matchless grace and the efficacy of His so-great salvation!

Water

Under the shade of great old mango trees can be seen the stone curbing of the open village well. A ramp has been built up on one side, and here stand the bullocks ready to pull the windlass and draw up the black skin full of water, which then empties into the trough beside the well. The water boy in dhoti, shirt, and turban, brown with dust, holds the rude rope lines. Then with a burst of song, a strange, minor cadence which he and the oxen understand, they start down the improvised slope, performing their monotonous but ever fascinating task.

This picture is duplicated in hundreds of villages. Much of Indian life and activity centers at the well. If the well is not deep and large, water may be drawn up in a bucket hand over hand by the women who come walking with their vessels on their heads, beautifully erect, maintaining that perfect poise and grace of posture which women who have access to taps and spigots seem to lose.

People cannot remain long in a village where water fails. The getting of sufficient water is a major concern to all this section of India. Therefore, to the progress and advancement of our missionary endeavors it also offers a primary problem.

Water, of course, is vital to the preservation of life. Men can live longer deprived of food than of water. But it is doubly necessary to the missionary who is undertaking to teach his converts the rudiments of genuine Christian living and practice, for the people to whom our mission has come in India have not yet learned the value of washing their bodies as we are accustomed to doing.

They must be taught the importance of keeping their children's eyes, noses, and hair clean, their faces and hands washed, and their bodies free from ashes and dirt. Furthermore, though even the low caste Hindus do wash their clothing in the bed of a stream and spread it out upon the ground or on low bushes to dry, the Christian converts must be taught to do their laundry more often. They must learn the value of soap and even to discriminate between what water is clean and what is foul.

An abundant supply of good water is especially essential for the schools, where children are being trained in proper hygiene and sanitation. It is also a prime necessity for the hospital and our various dispensaries. Non-Christians have little conception of water as an antiseptic against possible infection, and their idea of cleansing a wound is to smear it with tar or cow dung. They must be taught the efficacy of water as a healing agent. The whole question of water, consequently, is a vital one.

Two wells owned by our Nazarene mission have never failed. One of these is on the property at Dhamandari near Buldana. Winding down the hill back of the Buddy McKay memorial chapel runs a rocky path. I followed it one day into the ravine and up the hummock until I came to the open well lined with stone. In the curbing are carved the date 1907 and the initials L. S. T. (L. S. Tracy). We are told that he was determined to solve the water problem in this area and, after prayer, decided upon this spot where digging was begun. Down through the rock they went to the depth of thirty feet, where natural drainage from sloping land provides water that in forty-four years has not failed.

The other well is at Dhad, where the Mogalai Primary Boarding School is now located. This well, under the shade of a large neem tree, is forty feet deep. It, too, has never run dry. On its curbing are the letters

"P. L. Beals." It is significant that the names of these two men should be inscribed thus on the sources of never-failing water. For twenty years Brother and Sister L. S. Tracy gave their best to India, setting a pattern and determining policies that have since proved to be sound and right. For thirty years now Brother and Sister P. L. Beals have carried on, casting an influence upon missions in India the force of which can never be reckoned. May these two wells not only be historic, but may they prove to be prophetic, that in this land where water shortage can become desperate the scriptures shall literally be fulfilled that "in the wilderness shall waters break out, and streams in the desert"; that "the parched ground shall become a pool, and the thirsty land springs of water."

With the exception of the two places already noted, water shortage was being felt throughout the entire Indian district at the time of our visit.

When we arrived at the mission station in Chikhli, we were first entertained at the Fritzlan bungalow. Upon going into the bathroom my eyes lighted upon this notice tacked upon the wall:

> *Dear Guest, we regret that a scanty rainfall and a dry well have produced an acute shortage of water. All our water must be hauled in bullock carts daily from the village. The houseboy will bring it to your room each morning in five-gallon tins. If you run out during the day, let your needs be known and they can be supplied from a drum in the kitchen.*

The sight of bullocks drawing a cart on which rested an iron barrel capable of holding one hundred and fifty imperial gallons (180 American gallons) was a familiar one. The normal average yearly rainfall for this part of India is thirty-five inches. Last year only nineteen inches fell. With yet four months to go before rain could be expected, the problem was serious. It was not only the Chikhli missionaries and their Indian helpers who were affected. The coeducational school, with two hundred and sixty-five boarding students, must also be provided for.

One well on the compound was sixty feet deep and twenty-five feet wide. Another was sixty feet deep and seven feet in diameter. There was also a bored well ninety feet deep which had a good windmill for pumping water. But the entire supply gave out this year six months before rainfall could normally be expected. It was taking six bullock cart loads at the cost of eight rupees ($1.75) a day to care for the needs of the Chikhli school and compound, and this did not include water for washing clothes.

The well at the Beals bungalow a quarter of a mile away was also dry, and they too had been hauling water each day for several months from the village well one mile away.

In Basim the situation was duplicated. There is a well on the mission property where the Bible school is located, but water in it was so low that only a little was being drawn each day by the Bible students. The supply was being augmented daily by loads brought in by bullock carts from Basim, a mile away. The cost of this was Rs. 5 ($1.10) per day.

At the hospital the situation was necessarily more critical. Here there are two wells twenty-five and sixty feet deep. One of them was completely dry, and the other supplied only a small amount of water for the household needs of those residing on the compound. All of the water for the hospital was brought in by bullock carts. Dr. Witthoff had it apportioned in the following manner:

To the nurses for cooking, washing,	
and bathing	28 4-gallon tins
Soiled linen	8 to 10 4-gallon tins
Orphans	8 to 10 4-gallon tins
Lavatories	16 4-gallon tins
Hospital (in addition to the above)	48 4-gallon tins

The cost was Rs. 12 ($2.65) a day. She cheerfully admitted it was her number-one headache in administration of hospital affairs. It is easy to see precious General Budget money trickle away through this uncalculated channel.

In Pusad a fine property was already in hand upon which a mission bungalow and dispensary are to be erected in the near future. Ground was broken for the project by Mr. Williamson on February 5, 1951. No delicate "garden implement" fluttering crepe paper was provided for the purpose, nor yet even a spade that could be called a spade. He was furnished an old-fashioned grubbing mattock and told to break ground. And break it he did, with both hands, and with back bent, and with a vigor which bespoke the ardor he felt for the undertaking! Water, here too, was a problem, but even since our visit a well has been dug and living water reached which insures the future of this station against drought. Praises be to God!

From the foregoing facts it was evident to the visiting General Superintendent, both from the standpoint of economy and efficiency, that the solution of this problem headed the list of the imperative needs for the India field. To this the missionary chairman and the council readily acceded, though it must be recognized that these heroic souls accept all their hardships with a certain resignation that prevents their complaining or becoming embittered over situations that in the homeland would be thought intolerable.

It appeared that several courses were open for the permanent solution of the problem, none of which were alternative. It may seem wise to employ them all in the improvement of the total picture.

First, the wells already dug could be deepened. It will be noted that numbers of them for purposes of economy were not, in the first place, dug to a great depth. By going on down from thirty to sixty or seventy-five feet much greater area for underground seepage would be gained.

The second possibility is suggested by the hope that, in the digging of new wells or by deepening those already dug, springs of living water would be found, which, both for purity and abundance of water, offer the highest type of well. The report is that Indian water prospectors do not prove reliable in locating underground springs. However, some of the village wells are supplied by such springs which even in years of severest drought have never failed. There are those among the missionaries who feel that, in response to prevailing prayer and the faith that will not be denied, God would be pleased to give some wells of living water. The successful location of living water at the Pusad station is an encouragement to our faith at this point.

The third possibility is that, by equipping the mission buildings with eaves troughs, rain water could be caught and stored in underground cisterns which would be built for the purpose. This would be of particular advantage to the hospital. The soft rain water would be an improvement for use in the sterilizer, where the lime content of the water in present use offers a problem of residue in the machine. Furthermore, at both hospital and schools, where there is much water used daily for personal washing and for laundry purposes, it would seem that the conservation of rain water would be a good plan. This would supply an immense amount of water yearly because of the heavy rainfall during the wet months. Dr. Witthoff secured an estimate that 900,000 gallons of water could be caught each rainy season from the roof of the present hospital building alone.

In the brief months since our visit, commendable progress in deepening some of the wells has already been made. The well at the Beals house has gone down to thirty feet and now has good water. The new well at the hospital has also been deepened from twenty-five to forty feet. The Dittmore Chapel at the Basim Bible School has been equipped with gutters and eaves troughs at a cost of Rs. 150 ($33.00), and the water caught, stored in the open well nearby. The rainfall in 1951 has been more plentiful (twenty-five inches), so that following this rainy season all the wells on the district are full. Everyone feels encouraged. But this joy is temporary. The whole situation must be changed so that even during the dry season, and especially in years of drought, our work will not be hindered or endangered.

Salvation is frequently referred to in God's Word under the symbolism of water, and many beautiful promises are given us to indicate His eagerness to supply this element so vital to the spiritual life of man. But it seems it would not be a wresting of scripture to claim some of them literally at this time when our work in India faces constant handicap because of the lack of an adequate physical water supply. These words from Isaiah 41:17-18, 20-21 were first quickened to Nurse Geraldine Chappell, and have since been made living to others.

When the poor and needy seek water, and there is none, and their tongue faileth for thirst, I the Lord will hear them, I the God of Israel will not forsake them. I will open rivers in high places, and fountains in the midst of the valleys. I will make the wilderness a pool of water, and the dry land springs of water, that they may see, and know, and consider, and understand together, that the hand of the Lord hath done this, and the Holy One of Israel hath created it. Produce your cause, saith the Lord; bring forth your strong reasons, saith the King of Jacob.

It is our part to make the facts known, to set forth the "strong reasons" for this pressing need. And then God will not fail His good promise! He will hear the cry of the thirsty and He will open up in the dry land springs of water!

Touring

That portion of India where the Nazarene mission operates boasts three seasons—the hot, the rainy, and the cool. During the hot season it is impossible to do much more than hold the ground already gained. Temperatures soar to 120 degrees Fahrenheit and beyond. The Indians themselves take refuge from the burning sun in the shelter of their mud houses. Work is suspended. Man and beast wait languidly for the cooling rains. Under doctor's orders, missionaries of every denomination depart for a part of this time to the hills. Some few hardy souls who have attempted to stay down in the plains have found their health seriously impaired for a year or longer. The months of March, April, May, and June compass this period.

Before the monsoon winds start to blow and the rains begin to fall, the missionaries return to their stations. The earth, parched with thirst, revives. Great cracks and fissures which have opened in the ground are healed. Trees put forth their leaves and fields become green. Crops are sown and life and beauty appear. In a normal season, approximately thirty-two inches of rain falls during the months of July, August, September, and October. The first of this season offers opportunity for effective effort in our churches and for aggressive evangelism in undeveloped areas. But it is plain to be seen that with so great precipitation in so short a space of time even main roads, built of mud and rocks, become dangerous and the tracks across fields and swollen streams which lead to more remote villages become absolutely impassable even for the compound gear of the heroic jeep.

One man of another mission returning from a tour of evangelism found that the trickling stream he had crossed on the way out had became a roaring flood by the time of his return. He thought he could make it, but when he reached the middle of the stream his jeep was swept from under him and he himself escaped drowning as by a miracle. Our own missionary, Bronell Greer, modestly tells that, forced on one occasion to abandon his touring outfit, he plunged into the waters of a swollen stream and swam across, so buffeted by the current that he arrived at the opposite bank several hundred yards downstream. His Indian man reluctantly followed the missionary's lead, carrying Greer's shoes, his watch, and his wallet across in his turban.

By process of elimination, therefore, it is easily discerned that the cool season offers the golden opportunity for district tours. This season begins roughly in November and lasts through December, January, and February. Before February is well begun the winds start to rise. Small eddies of dust may be seen swirling across an open field or advancing toward one on the road. As the days progress the heat becomes more noticeable. Like a gray haze, dust lies upon the lowlands, billows after every bullock cart upon the road; and when an occasional bus or motor lorry passes, it rises in a blinding, suffocating cloud. Some of the missionaries wear masks tied over mouth and nose when on tour. Others, more annoyed by this precaution, choose the major of the two evils and breathe in the dust. All suffer to greater or lesser degree from sinus infection due to this hazard to eyes, nose, and throat. They accept it without complaint. Like malaria, typhoid, diphtheria, and dysentery, it is included in a missionary's consecration.

I noticed a large black and blue spot on Dr. Witthoff's arm. "Well, Doctor," I said, "I see you must have been pinching yourself just like I have done since arriving in India to make sure we are really here."

"Oh, that," she laughed. "I guess I must have gotten too much dust a few days ago. My sinuses were infected and I was running a temperature, so I gave myself a shot of penicillin. It's nothing at all." She had not missed one hour of work and had just told us with shining face that "she was making no sacrifice to be in India."

All of these soldiers of the Cross look forward to touring, but it is not because it offers them an easier existence than they would have by remaining on their stations. In America, we Nazarenes enjoy an overland trip from Kansas City to St. Louis; from Albany, New York, to Portland, Maine; or from Walla Walla, Washington, to Nampa, Idaho. We know it entails packing our suitcases with our personal belongings and climbing into the Chevie, the Pontiac, or the Buick, and setting out on a superhighway for our destination. We know we can either spend the night with some Nazarenes en route or stop at a good hotel or motor court. We know we can usually buy our meals in clean, appetizing eating places. We know that when we are thirsty we can secure safe drinking water or iced bottle drinks. When we need gas, if we have used our heads at all, there will be a convenient Shell or Mobil Gas or Standard pump available.

But in India planning to tour is a bit more complicated. One must carry his house, his furniture, his food, his stove, his cooking utensils, his drinking water, his lighting system, and extra gasoline. He must take several vehicles to carry his load, and several Indian helpers to assist him in setting up the equipment or to remain with part of the load when this must be temporarily abandoned.

Brother Beals is system personified, and I did catch sight of his typewritten "trip list." The first was "Personal," containing items of clothing and toilet requisites. The second was "Miscellaneous," and included:

1. Cameras and films
2. Light meters
3. Tripod
4. Projector, screen, cord, film, oil and tools, spare reel
5. P.A. system, horns, battery, cords for battery, and
   110 wiring and connection, light bulbs, mikes,
   and records
6. Flash and bulb
7. Torches, pen and ink
8. Glasses and case
9. Stationery and money

The third was a "Travel" list:

1. Water bottle, thermos
2. Bedding, nets, sheets, pillows
3. Passport, driver's license, police registration
4. Keys, brief case, account books, money sack, address
   book, and maps

The fourth was titled "Touring":

1. Tent, stakes, poles, rope
2. Stove
3. Lanterns, spirits, kerosene
4. Tiffin basket, tin openers, cups, saucers, plates, cut-
   lery, napkins, tablecloths, toothpicks, dish towels.
   cloths, soap, matches
5. Frying pan, cooking pan, teakettle and strainer, cot-
   feepot, sharp knife
6. Wash basin and pitcher, cup
7. Food, tin goods, soup, milk, butter, frying grease,
   salt, pepper, sugar, tea, coffee, bread, jam, fruit,
   porridge, vegetables, nuts, eggs
8. Dishes, porridge dishes
9. Medicine kit
10. Spare lock
11. Table and chairs

One of the high spots of our visit to India was our trip to the Mogalai, into the domain of the Nizam of Hyderabad, one of the richest rulers in India—in fact, one of the wealthiest men in the world.

Driving the 1950 Chevie was Leslie Fritzlan, missionary chairman, and one of the finest men God ever called to be a missionary. Beside him sat Mr. Williamson, looking like a missionary himself in Indian topee and borrowed cotton suit. Assisting me in driving from the back seat was Mrs. Beals, whose sparkling humor and wonderful spirit make any occasion a delight; while Brother Beals, who was planning and executing the trip, was first in the back seat, then in the front, an able general, a perfect host—tenderness, courtesy, grace, and saintliness all in one. The hearts of the Bealses are in India, and it was a thrill to them to take us to one of their most needy fields.

We made quite a pretentious showing as we started out. The two loud-speaker horns and several bedrolls were in the carrier on top of the Chevrolet. The trunk was full. Following came the red jeep carrying Samuel Bhujbal and three Indian assistants, while attached to the jeep was a trailer, loaded with cots, stove, cooking utensils, and canned goods. Brother Bhujbal was armed with a rifle, which he held erect beside him. We weren't quite sure what he expected to see—a tiger, a deer, a fox, or a hare. Whatever it was, he did not see it!

The aspect of the terrain altered somewhat as we proceeded. The land became more rugged and mountainous. The Mogalai have ever been a warlike people, and remains of high mud walls surround all their villages. Most of them are entered through a great gate and some were further protected by a moat and inner gate.

Our first stop was at the village of Deulgaonraja. Here we have no organized church, but we do own a small building made of mud with *shane* (cow dung) floor and with windows and a door opening on the street side. There are a number of Christian believers here, and they were joined this day in welcoming us by a congregation three miles distant in Pimpalgoon village, who with their pastor, Prasadrao Manerikar, had walked in to Deulgaonraja. As we approached the village, the minister stepped forward and stopped the car. The Bealses and the Williamsons alighted, and were welcomed with garlands, songs, and expressions of joy. Then with the minister leading, a procession formed, moving down the main street to the church. First, came a few musicians with pipe and drum and high-sounding cymbals; next, the visitors surrounded by the Christian congregation, singing songs of joy and triumph, their bodies moving to the rhythm, and pausing now and again to shout, *"Yesu Masiki Jay."* ("Victory to Jesus, the Messiah!") I thought it must have been something like that when Israel advanced singing before the ark of the Lord. Brother Fritzlan in the Chevie and the Indian Christians in the jeep, with the trailer, brought up the rear.

But that was not all. The demonstration caused no small stir in the village. We were joined by groups of children, many of them with a younger brother or sister on their hips and all bearing the marks of Hinduism— rings in ears or nose or the red *kunka* powder or caste tattoo on the forehead of the older girls. Boys and young men also joined the group in numbers, with several older ones as well. A few pye-dogs completed the procession.

When we reached the little church and the Christians were seated on the floor, as many non-Christians as could possibly squeeze in did so, while the door and windows were filled to overflowing by the rest. The impressive thing about it all was the courage and holy enthusiasm shown by this little band of believers in witnessing for Christ in a village where the gospel was as yet so little known. After a good service with a message from those wonderful words, "Come unto me, all ye that labour and are heavy laden, and I will give you rest," we proceeded on our way, with many a backward glance at those faithful few who stood surrounded by their Hindu brethren, their hands still raised in farewell salaams.

Our stop for lunch afforded us a complete surprise, for, having passed through the larger town of Jalna and the city of Arangabad, we did not pull off the road and start pitching camp as I had anticipated. Instead, we stopped before a very beautiful building of Spanish-type architecture and fronted by beautiful flower gardens. It proved to be the state hotel of Hyderabad, and here we were served an excellent lunch, both menu and food being in English. From the upper veranda was a splendid vista. On the left was the old fort Daulatabad and before us the Bibi-ka-mak-bara tomb, a replica of the Taj Mahal at Agra. The Elura and the Ajunta caves are also in the region, and this hotel on the British plan is an added attraction to accommodate visitors who come to these places of interest.

After lunch, Brother Beals went off on an errand of apparent secrecy. When he returned he was bubbling with joy, and time proved that he had had a favorable answer to his request that we be permitted to spend the night in the guesthouse of the Nizam of Hyderabad located near the Ajunta caves. Two comfortable nights in this commodious and well-furnished shelter, with the privilege of preparing and serving our meals in the spacious dining hall attended by the servants of the house, took from the trip much of the rigor that the missionaries experience on similar excursions.

While in the locality we counted it a privilege to visit two of the historic caves of India. The Elura caves date from at least the thirteenth century. They are excavations made from above down into the solid rock, in commemoration of the deities of Hinduism. The Ajunta caves are distinctive in that upon their walls are painted with artistic skill of a very definite rank, scenes and reproductions pertaining to the worship of Buddha. Our guide through the Ajunta caves was the curator himself. He is responsible for the management of the guesthouse, so we had made his acquaintance upon our arrival there. He informed us in jovial mood and in very good English that he was the representative of Lord Buddha. Brother Beals lost no opportunity to make it known that his guest was the representative of the Lord Jesus Christ.

Later, while viewing the caves, he again offered us the chance to witness. He suggested that someone sing a song to demonstrate the beautiful echo in one particular excavation. After a pause in which no one responded, Mr. Williamson began and the others of our Christian band joined in singing:

> *When I survey the wondrous cross*
> *On which the Prince of Glory died,*
> *My richest gain I count but loss,*
> *And pour contempt on all my pride.*

Hindus, Moslems, and Buddhists in the company stood in respectful silence until the last echo had died away. "Pride—pride—pride!" The word itself seemed to condemn this religion of Buddha which it had here sought to extol. The cross, the emblem of suffering and shame, is the symbol of the Prince of Glory. We follow in His train.

"Out of devotion these caves were made," the curator had said. Out of devotion *our* religion must be promulgated, not in excavations in stone, not in paintings of oil upon the rock, but in the living sacrifice of those who profess His name. The missionaries of the Church of the Nazarene in India are giving the full measure of devotion. How do we in the homeland appear as God takes account of our poured-out love and loyalty?

The village of Shillod was our next stop in the Mogalai. It is without any Christian band or witness. When the men began at dusk to set up the loud-speakers and the equipment for showing the slides depicting the life of Jesus Christ, the Messiah, a crowd began to gather. Police permission had been obtained and they were there to see what went on. Instructed through the loud-speaker to do so, the people sat cross-legged on the ground, as is always the Indian custom; or with knees clasped in front of their bodies, as is common among the men. There they were—children of every age and description, the younger ones clothed in a single garment; men with turbaned heads denoting as a rule the better class, the older ones carrying a staff or stick and some among them a lighted lantern. Toward the back was quite a group of women drawn from their homes by the unusual attraction.

One person asked Mrs. Beals what the pictures would be about. When her reply was, "About Jesus Christ," the answer came, "Oh, we heard about Him once before. Someone came a year ago and told about Him then. They have never been back since." It had been just about a year before that representatives of the Nazarene mission had visited Shillod.

This evening they sat breathless as Brother Bhujbal told the story of Jesus as the pictures were shown. An old man near me watched with consuming interest as the story unfolded. Once someone hunting a place to sit down obstructed his vision for a moment. Distress filled his face and he raised his stick as though to strike, so eager did he seem not to miss one detail.

Twice during the telling of the precious story a tremor like a universal sigh swept across that audience of fifteen hundred to two thousand people, and was gone. Once was when the Baby Jesus in the manger was shown, so pure, so holy, coming to earth to take upon Him our likeness. The other was when He hung upon the cross, dying for our sins and theirs. Brother Fritzlan says he has never known it to fail with an Indian audience hearing the Christian message for the first time. It is the distinctive wonder of our religion. He "took upon him the form of a servant, and was made in the likeness of men . . . . he humbled himself, and became obedient unto death, even the death of the cross."

When the story was ended, it was announced over the loud-speaker that Bible portions would be sold. Those people fairly mobbed the boy who was prepared to sell the Gospels, so eager were they to obtain one. They laid hands on the books and would have torn them apart had not the police and the missionaries rescued the salesman.

It is probable that a mission station to the memory of Dr. H. V. Miller may be located at Shillod in the near future. One purpose of our visit was to inspect possible sites. It would not be too soon.

The following morning we were scheduled for a service at Bhipur. Early, Mr. Williamson began inquiring what time the people were expecting us as nervously as if he were intending to convene a District Assembly in America. But the missionaries laughingly reminded him that the Indian people were never in a hurry and that, if they arrived before we did, they would wait indefinitely. The Chevie had to be abandoned some few miles from the village; so, leaving a man to watch it, we all piled into the jeep with Samuel Bhujbal on the hood, and Kondu, the cook, in the trailer, and started off across a cotton field to Bhipur. We traversed the bed of a stream, now nearly dry, just before the village came into view. The jeep stood on its side as we bumped up the opposite bank, but still Mr. Williamson complained that the ride had really been too soft. As we negotiated the last hill, the fine pastor, Robert Irshid, and the Christian people came out to greet us.

We could see at a glance that this was one of the most primitive villages we had yet visited. The sun blazed down on the mud houses. Up the narrow, dusty village street women paused to stare at us, their earthen waterpots poised on their heads. Little children, and older ones as well, gathered round us to gaze and to giggle at our foreign ways and clothing.

To this village just a few years before, five of our young preachers had come on their bicycles to tell the people for the first time the gospel story. We saw the little thatched bamboo shelter where they had lived those first difficult days. But a Christian community was the result. We now own property where a church building is to be erected. However, this day our only protection was a bamboo thatch placed upon poles before the preacher's mud house and forming a sort of arbor. It was so low that neither Mr. Williamson nor Mr. Bhujbal could stand to speak. But the Christian people, neat and smiling, crowded in as close as they could possibly sit. Usually in an Indian congregation the men are on the right hand of the building and the women on the left. It always impressed me as a sort of premature dividing of the sheep from the goats. But on this day the women crowded in close to the wall of the house on the right to escape more completely the rays of the sun. The men followed, while the Hindus filled in all other space and stood or squatted about.

The marks of sin and ignorance perhaps were greater upon this group than upon any we saw while in India. Two boys less than twelve years of age were stricken with blindness. One little fellow's eyes were sightless. The other had the use of only one. They were no doubt offspring of syphilitic parents or were simply the victims of the carelessness and filth so common among unenlightened people. Tiny babies in their Hindu mothers' laps before us could scarcely open their eyes because of the infection already at work in them. Flies crawled unheeded over their faces, and the little things would take their tiny fists and try to brush them away. A simple argyrol-tipped swab doubtless would have cleared them up in a few days. In the crowd were older ones wearing the bright red or purple fez denoting they were the children of Mohammedan parents. This cap was the single article of clothing except for bracelets on arms and ankles and a chain about the waist. Some old men with sticks for canes hobbled in. Numbers of young men and older ones listened attentively for a time; then, as is so frequent with an untaught congregation, they would get up and move away, perhaps to come back and sit down again before the service was over.

Today there was no musical instrument, not even the little lap organ pumped from the back as we sometimes had in our services, nor the skin-covered basket-like drums. But the minister raised a hymn and the people sang. Then there was a prayer, and garlands and a welcome for the visitors, which beautiful ceremony was never once omitted in India. Then it was announced there were converts to baptize. This sacrament is a very significant one in this land of heathen religion. It is not administered to new converts. These must first prove during a probationary period that they have been truly regenerated and that they intend to take the way with the Lord. In every case an earnest effort is made to bring both father and mother into the church at the same time, thus keeping the family unit intact. Baptism sets one apart definitely as a Christian, and its reception sometimes is a signal for persecution to begin.

The questions that Brother Bhujbal put to these applicants were very telling. He said to the father:

"Are you becoming a Christian of your own will and accord?"

"If you were offered money to go back to Hinduism, would you accept it?"

"If the Hindus refuse to let you get water at the well, will you still keep true?"

"If they drive you from the village, will you deny your Lord?"

Then turning to the woman he asked:

"Is anyone forcing you to become a Christian?"

"Has your husband beaten you and told you you must do so?"

"Will you be true even if the women of the village laugh at you?"

He then searched the older son, eleven or twelve years of age, with similar appropriate questions. The bright eyes and face of the lad seemed to comprehend even more the significance of the step the family was taking than perhaps either the father or mother. I have since breathed a prayer that God would lay His hand on that boy and on the younger brother beside him, and make them shine for His glory and the advancement of His cause in India. It would mean much to a child to leave the gods and the ways of other boys, and start upon a new and untried path alone. And yet he is not alone, for God's promises are just as sure for that boy in the heart of India as they are for any of us.

The message that day was "Follow Peace and Holiness," and the Lord was there to bless His word. Five or six responded to the call to seek the Lord as Saviour or Sanctifier. There was also talk and planning for the camp meeting which in a few weeks was to open in the Mogalai.

After service the pastor's wife proudly showed us her home. It was a two-room dwelling of mud walls and *shane* floor. In the front room there were the cord beds and several tin boxes or small trunks where clothing and bedding are kept. There were one or two pictures of religious significance cut out and fastened to the wall. In the kitchen was a small cupboard in which were some brass and earthen dishes, and in a corner the little built-up shelter of clay where fire was kept for cooking. That was all. But it was clean and neat. The children showed the marks of cleanliness and care, and we felt God's presence in that humble home. It is an example to the entire village. God bless that faithful pastor and his wife!

Dinner that day was in the open, down among the trees of the "jungle," and a good one it was too. It was supplemented by a bountiful helping of chicken curry from the pastor's home, for our Christians are hospitable and showed us every kindness. As we climbed back into the jeep, Christians and Hindus followed us down the road to the edge of the village. I wondered if this was an Indian farewell, but discovered that it also had its utilitarian purposes; for, when even the jeep couldn't make it in the heavy sand by the riverbank, all hands heaved ho and we were soon on our way.

It was a never-to-be-forgotten trip. Our hearts had been deeply stirred as we saw needs before unrealized and the power of the gospel before uncomprehended. Night was falling and we grew quiet as the twilight brought its contemplative mood. Bodies were weary and minds oppressed with the burden of India's need, and but for the encouragement of the Spirit our souls would have faltered at the enormity of the task.

And then through the gathering darkness lights blazed out—the lights of home. We turned off the dusty road where the tinkling bells of the bullocks and the creaking of the wheels of the carts were as endless as India's longing, and walked into the haven of the mission bungalow. Mrs. Fritzlan and Mrs. Blackman had a fine, hot supper waiting for us; and after we had eaten and refreshed ourselves, we covered the brief distance remaining to the home of Brother and Sister Beals.

This new cement-block house with its painted plaster walls and stone floors is roomy and comfortable. It is airy and light. It is well planned to provide workrooms, eating, sleeping, and living rooms. It is the nicest home they have ever lived in, in thirty years of married life. Yet it cost but five thousand dollars. They showed us through with pleasure, and our hearts rejoiced with them. But when we came to the study where Brother Beals displayed his fine fluorescent light, a gift from the Northwest District W.F.M.S., we had no words to say; for he added lightly: "If I had had this all these years, maybe my eyes would be better. They were never too good, and I worked so long at my books by the light of a kerosene lantern that they nearly gave out."

Yes, our missionaries must tour. They must go out where humanity suffers and sins and dies. They must rescue the perishing and care for the dying. But lest both heart and body break under the pressure they must be able to come back, when evening falls, to the quiet, the security, the peace, and the haven of a Christian home.

The Spearhead
Of Missionary Progress

The evangelists always march in the front line of an advancing missionary enterprise. They are the trail blazers. Some of them may have been doctors, like David Livingstone, but in their hearts has burned the passion to evangelize the masses of people who dwell in the land to which they have been called. Others may have been teachers and translators, like William Carey of India, or Esther Carson Winans, missionary to the Aguaruna Indians of Peru. However, the deathless desire to make Christ known to those who never heard His name spoken was the motivation of their lives of supreme devotion. Missionaries who have not possessed the vision and burden of an evangelist have not long remained missionaries. They have either failed on the field or have for one reason or another returned to the more comfortable lives of their homeland after a brief term of service.

There are many tasks to be performed on the mission field. Persons of widely varied skills and gifts must be sent forth. But whether they be mechanics, farmers, bookkeepers, architects, builders, printers, translators, nurses, doctors, teachers, administrators, pastors, or evangelists, all must have the consuming passion to turn men from darkness to light and from the power of Satan unto God, that they may receive forgiveness of sins and inheritance among them that are sanctified by faith in Jesus. Furthermore, all their efforts in whatever phase of the work they may be engaged must converge at the point of evangelizing the people of the land to which they have been sent by God's appointment. The arguments advanced by many, among whom was Mahatma Gandhi, that to use educational and medical means for the purpose of evangelism is unethical, are all invalid in the mind of a God-called missionary who believes that without Christ all men are lost and undone, without God and without hope in the world. And this conviction alone will keep the work of Christian missions from languishing in stalemate and stagnation.

Evangelism is required to accomplish the conversion of men, in order that God's regenerating grace and power may condition their minds to receive Christian education. Paul declared to the Corinthians long ago, "The natural man receiveth not the things of the Spirit of God: for they are foolishness unto him: neither can he know them, because they are spiritually discerned" (I Cor. 2:14). Only the renewing of the mind by a miracle of moral and spiritual transformation can make that mind ready to receive the knowledge of God and spiritual things.

It is also necessary for us to comprehend the fact that no process of education can be saved from becoming formal and secular unless it be fused with the spirit of evangelism. Education that does not have for its dominant purpose the redemption of men from the power and pollution of sin, and from the bondage of superstition and error, will soon be concerned only with the betterment of living conditions in this world and will lose sight of the fact that, though a man gain the whole world, if he lose his own soul it will profit him nothing. A knowledge of the worth of an immortal soul must be taught, and that alone will keep education evangelistic and Christian.

The genius of the whole Christian movement from Pentecost until now has been the evangelistic spirit. The responsibility of the Christian Church is summarized in the Great Commission. Without that sense of obligation that characterized the Church of the first century, Christianity ceases to be Christian. It becomes, even in the minds of its devotees, only one of the world's religions. It loses its distinctive character. It is no longer a vital force for human redemption. Its revolutionary power is dissipated and its advocates become victims rather than victors. In the present conflict between Christianity and communism, which is rising to a new pitch of intensity day by day, only a virile, vigorous, aggressive church, fired by an evangelistic passion, can hope to gain the victory.

It is unsafe to give the fruits and by-products of Christianity which are produced in a Christian civilization to unregenerated peoples. If they have these benefits without the knowledge of God in personal salvation, they will in all probability remain content to do without that new life which can come only to those supernaturally born of the Spirit. Thus we may do them the injury of giving them temporal blessings without giving them life eternal. In other words, we will give them satisfaction in their carnal security that will hinder rather than accomplish their eternal salvation.

If we do give the fruits of Christian civilization to men without leading them to a knowledge of Christ in personal salvation, they will no doubt take those means which we have placed within their reach to accomplish our destruction. Such ironical turn of the tables even now threatens us.

It is not our purpose to convert the Orientals to our Western way of life. We are to convert them to Christ. They must know Him in personal experience whom to know is life eternal. Therefore the means and motives of evangelism must always be scrutinized and evaluated in the light of God's love revealed by the death of His Son on Calvary's cross. All who go as missionaries and all who send them forth must be actuated by love for Christ and those for whom He died. Every means used to win converts to Christianity must be according to love. Mohammedanism is evangelistic, but it is right according to that doctrine to make converts by the sword. Christianity has suffered some all-but-mortal defeats when carnal means and motives have been allowed a place in its promotion. Witness the conquest of Latin America by those who justified any means to accomplish their ends.

On the evening of February 19, 1951, we set out by car from Buldana to drive sixty-eight miles to Bhusaval to catch our train for Bombay. Due to a full day of scheduled appointments, we started a few minutes later than planned. Other factors, such as bullock carts, clouds of dust, police inspections, and the like, did not help us make up lost time. Therefore, just as we came down the steps to the station platform we saw our train slowly moving away. We were adjusting our minds to the idea of waiting two hours for the next train (it proved to be three hours) when Brother Weldon Franklin recognized Rev. Fred Schlander, a Christian and Missionary Alliance man, walking along the platform. They greeted one another cordially. By the time Brother Franklin had introduced us to his friend, Brother Beals had appeared. Then the two veteran missionaries went into an affectionate embrace. They had been friends since the days of their language study together, but this was their first meeting in six years.

When Missionary Schlander knew of our enforced wait for the next train, he insisted we come over to his bungalow for a visit and some tea. We consented without reluctance. There around his table we heard the story of the beginning of what later became our Nazarene mission in Buldana. Rev. M. D. Wood and his wife had gone there under appointment by the Christian and Missionary Alliance board. That fact was even unknown to Brother

Beals. A few years after his arrival in Buldana in the year 1899, Rev. M. D. Wood had some disagreement with his board and withdrew from the church. He then identified himself with the Pentecostal Association of Churches in America and opened another mission in Buldana. For a time the two groups worked in the same town with an understanding that a certain street should be the dividing line between them. A little later the Christian and Missionary Alliance Mission withdrew to occupy other territory, leaving Buldana to Brother Wood and his associates. Several other missionaries joined the mission, and in some respects the work moved forward. In 1907, when the union of the Pentecostal Association of Churches with the Church of the Nazarene was effected, the Buldana mission was incorporated into the united body as one of its missionary projects. In 1906, however, Mr. Wood had reached another point of disagreement with the board in America. He insisted on having sole control of all mission funds without reference to the home board or the other missionaries on the field. Since such a policy could not be accepted, one night while unsuspecting missionaries slept, Mr. and Mrs. Wood, with two other missionaries, left Buldana by bullock cart train, taking with them nearly one hundred people, including every Indian Christian—boys, girls, Bible women, and preachers—except one, who remained loyal. They took all the property that was conveniently movable and all cash in hand except seventy-five cents.

This seemed like a staggering blow, and it was. But it is possible that God has overruled the apparent tragedy to give us a stronger and larger work in India today, for this exodus brought about a change of policy as well as of leadership. Brother Wood had concentrated all his efforts, and those of the missionaries and workers under his guidance, in Buldana. Much attention was given to work among orphans. He adopted all of them and gave them his name. It is still possible to find those bearing his name who are fullblood Indians. After the departure of the four missionaries to which reference has already been made, there were five left. Mrs. Ella Perry was a woman of mature years, all the others were youthful beginners; four of the five were women. The only man among them was Rev. L. S. Tracy, who was in his early twenties. But if he was young in years, he was mature in vision and judgment. With courage and faith in God he assumed the leadership of the mission, bereft of all its converts and movable assets. He said, "To come within two miles of the people and fail to reach them is as blameworthy as to remain at home ten thousand miles away." Therefore, he inaugurated the program of systematic visitation of villages which has been carried on until this present day. Thus the policy of giving first attention to evangelism, with institutions secondary and auxiliary, was begun, and has been fully justified by its fruits throughout the years. It is also interesting to recall that when the General Board purchased the property in Basim in 1935 there came with it some of those converts and workers who had departed from Buldana on that eventful night twenty-nine years before.

While the program in India today includes schools, dispensaries, and a hospital for women and children, yet one readily finds that the first thing in the policy is evangelism. And he also discovers that every missionary —whether evangelist, teacher, nurse, doctor, or administrator—has the soul of an evangelist and is actively seeking to make his work serve the primary purpose of saving souls by bringing them to Christ, the Light of the World.

The means of transportation in use by the missionaries of the present are quite improved. Main roads are usable for automobiles. When the cart roads must be traveled to reach the villages, a jeep is a big improvement for speed and comfort over the bullock cart. In fact, I said repeatedly while in India, "A jeep is the missionaries' best friend." And even as the means of transportation have improved, so have the methods of approach to the people been brought up to date.

Rev. P. L. Beals, by his own request, has been assigned to the work of evangelization. After many years as chairman of the Mission Council, he desired to spend what he expects to be his last term in India in promoting revivals and entering new fields. Rev. Bronell Greer is also devoting his full time to the work of evangelism. Both of these men have public-address systems by which they can make their voices heard distinctly by everyone in a village of average size. They also have beautiful slides which portray the story of the life and death of Jesus Christ. They move into a village and let the news be scattered around that they will show pictures of the life of Christ that evening. By the time they have their little Onan electric plant operating and the equipment ready, the darkness will have gathered and a great milling crowd will surround them. When the pictures begin, those village people sit on the ground and there in breathless silence watch and listen as the pictures are shown and "the greatest story ever told" is related in their native tongue. When the pictures are finished, Gospel portions are sold and tracts distributed. By the time it is all over, it may be anywhere between midnight and 3:00 a.m. The missionary may spend a week or more in a village, repeating the program with variations night after night. Brother Greer says that if he were to spend two weeks in each village in his territory, which is approximately half the district, it would take him forty-two years to contact them all.

This, of course, is only the opening wedge. It is the first step in reaching the masses of India. After this introduction there must be a follow-up. Some of our lady missionaries, like Sisters Beals, Blackman, and Freeman, go and deal personally with the women, who are more backward than men in responding to the light. Then a band of young preachers from the Bible school or those who have already finished their training will move into a village to stay for a number of weeks and even months to preach and visit and pray until a nucleus of believers is finally ready to come out boldly and be baptized. Then a national pastor is appointed. He may be denied a place to live or the right to get water from the village well, but somehow he will overcome these obstacles and stay on till a church is formed. Even then it is not easy. The revival fires must be kept burning; special meetings with a national evangelist or district superintendent or a missionary must be conducted. In spite of all, some will falter and go back to Hinduism. Others will backslide and go into sin. But God, by His marvelous grace, does bring many through to lives of strength, beauty, and fruitful service.

On a Sunday morning we had a service at Manabai, one of our older and better village churches. There is the chapel erected to the memory of Rev. R. G. Codding. It is a simple stone building with a *shane* floor. I preached with God's help. Several men and women came to pray. One was an old layman who in the early years of the church had quarreled with his brother (both of them were members of the church) until they almost defeated the church. Now that the brother was dead he was there asking God's forgiveness. Another was a young man who had been a trusted worker at the school in Chikhli, but he had committed awful sin and had been discharged. He asked God and the missionaries and the church to forgive him. The third old man with gray hair had been a preacher for twenty-five years, but he had taken to drink. His wife had died of a broken heart. His sons preached to their father about his sins. He said he awakened to the fact that he should be helping them in the Christian way when, in fact, they were dealing with him, a backslider. He was reclaimed, asked forgiveness, and at the camp professed to be sanctified. Thus it is seen that the work of evangelization in India has its varied problems and setbacks, just as it does in America.

The climax of a year's work is reached in the annual camp meeting. The first Jungle Camp of 1932 marked an epoch in the history of the Nazarene mission in India. The Pentecost that came then has never been forgotten. Its effect has been felt in all these nineteen years that have passed. This year witnessed the largest camp ever held. More than eight hundred men, women, and children were living on the grounds. They slept on the ground in little stalls made of bamboo mats. They cooked on open fires in or just outside those enclosures. The nights were so chilly that the fires had to be kept burning all night. In the tabernacle, the walls and roof of which were made of bamboo mats supported by bamboo poles, the people gathered to sing and pray and listen to the gospel message. Many were seeking God at the altar. Few if any services, either day or night, saw no one at the place of prayer. The high peak came on Sunday morning when forty to fifty seekers prayed through to victory after a message on the sufferings of Christ.

The camp meeting is now an established institution in India. It is the high point of each year to our national Christians and to the missionaries as well. It is only six days in duration, but its effect abides all the year through. They need a camp site and some buildings of simple construction. They have three thousand dollars laid by to make the purchase of the land. In a few minutes they subscribed 2,000 rupees toward the project, and had they been given more time would have gone on to make it four or five thousand. In addition to the amount subscribed for the new campground they exceeded all previous offerings for camp expenses, giving over 800 rupees. To them a rupee is many times our dollar, though it is worth only about twenty-two cents.

This program of evangelism has resulted in the establishment of twenty-five churches with three more ready to organize. There are at least two thousand baptized Christians. We had the privilege of baptizing about thirty-five of them. There are many secret believers and inquirers who are near the Kingdom. There is an organized indigenous church, with an Indian district superintendent, and all the churches having national pastors. They carried forward a district assembly in an orderly fashion. With no missionaries voting, one hundred ballots were cast for district superintendent. Brother Samuel Bhujbal was elected to succeed himself on the first ballot. In a land where there is 85 to 90 per cent illiteracy, only a few needed help to prepare their ballots, even when a long list was presented with many different nominees for the various positions.

I asked several of the national leaders what would happen if the missionaries should be compelled to leave India now. They all declared they would carry on in the tradition, doctrine, and spirit of the Church of the Nazarene. It is my opinion that in no mission field do we have a stronger national church than in India, and there are few to equal it.

During the camp I read from *India's Open Door,* by P. L. Beals, the following paragraphs:

> One touring season Mr. Tracy, feeling he could get closer to the people if he dressed more like them, donned an Indian turban and another type of clothes, and, taking a roll of blankets, a brass plate and cup, an umbrella and some Gospels started on a three-week trek in company with two Indian preachers. They went through the district on foot, stopping at the native inns—merely places of shelter without beds or food—where they sat around the smoky fires to talk and preach to the people who gathered there. Living creatures

kept them awake by night and the tropical sun beat upon their heads by day. They finally reached a place called Anwa, located in an Indian state about thirty miles from Buldana. This was the home of some Hindus who had previously shown some interest in Christianity. But the people did not receive Mr. Tracy and his party, and those whom they had come to see were "conveniently away." The people of the village made no attempt to give shelter but let them stay outside under a tree between the village and the river.

Mr. Tracy, in response to our request for this story said, "I remember that it was bitterly cold (for India) and that when I took a bath I put up some blankets between two carts to keep out the wind and took my bath after dark. I had a native bed [they are very short and also 'lively'—P. L. B.] which someone had lent me from the village. The day we were there was Sunday and as I sat on the edge of the bed I thought of the Sunday mornings when as a boy in the country I went to Sunday school and church away off in Canada, then of the experiences of the past weeks in the villages and the rejection in this village in the heart of India. I sat there and prayed and wept for a long while. My feelings were mingled. They were partly of joy that I could be in the service of the Lord away out here in the heart of old Indian heathenism and that He had called me from the farm and the plow and brought me to the extremity of the earth; they were also of disappointment that the people were not receiving the gospel; and they were partly what Jesus must have felt when He wept over Jerusalem. As I was playing the mouth organ I had bought in an Indian bazar I stumbled on the refrain, 'And when the battle's over we shall wear a crown.' Just then the Lord came and comforted my heart and made me assured that He would give us final victory there." And that is just what actually happened in Anwa.

One of the writer's first touring experiences was when, in company with Rev. F. Arthur Anderson, he made this same trip to Anwa—a trip made many times since. Mrs. Beals three years later had the privilege of being the first white woman to visit this part of our territory.

We are happy to say that this very section where the enemy tried so hard to discourage Mr. Tracy and make him think there was no use, is today one of the most fruitful parts of our entire Nazarene field. As many or more people are coming to Christ here as in any other area. And I doubt not that some of these are the same ones who seemed so unconcerned that memorable day when the Lord opened the windows of heaven upon Brother Tracy's soul. Many today can testify as one recent uneducated convert from the outcasts in that area did when he said in his initial testimony to the saving power of His new-found Christ, "A saved man is one whose sack of sins has all been spilled out." Yes, God was true to the assurance of victory given to Brother Tracy that day in Anwa.

As I sat on the platform on that last Sunday morning and saw the great crowd that was assembled and observed their clean faces, combed hair, clear eyes and felt the warmth of their spiritual fervor, I said in my heart, "I wish dear Brother Tracy could see what I witness today." But then I remembered that probably he does, with clearer vision even than my own. And I rejoice that Brother and Sister Beals were there to see the fruit of their thirty years of arduous, sacrificial toil.

There have been some outstanding trophies of grace. There is Kondu, Brother and Sister Beals's cook, a faithful Christian of many years, a man with a shining face and testimony, and a man of prayer and with a family that he has reared in the Christian fold. Again I quote from *India's Open Door*:

Another great epoch took place in 1919 on the eve of Mr. and Mrs. Fritzlan's departure for America after thirteen years of continuous service for him and eight for her. As a result of some meetings conducted by Mr. Tracy and Mr. Fritzlan several members of the robber caste had professed to be saved. A short time later, soon after Mr. Tracy and family had left on furlough, Mr. Fritzlan was startled one day to see his new Christians passing by the bungalow with handcuffs on their wrists as they were being led to the jail by the police. Upon investigation he learned that a big robbery had been committed the night before in a nearby village and that these men had been seized on general principles because of their past record; for all had been in jail, some a number of times, and two at least, had been transported one or more times to the Andaman Islands (India's

Alcatraz) in the Bay of Bengal for seven-year periods. They had all made their living for years by robbery and we have no doubt that some of them had human blood on their hands; a notorious band indeed.

While Mr. Fritzlan was talking to the head police official of Buldana District this officer said to Mr. Fritzlan, "Every time these men serve their sentences and are released from jail they commit greater depredations than ever before. As far as the police are concerned they are a hopeless lot. But now that they are interested in Christianity we are willing to give them a chance if you will take them into your care." Mr. Fritzlan had enough faith in the transforming power of the gospel of Christ to take the risk—and risk it was—for he took these men together with their families and gave them rooms in his back yard. Here they were when we arrived in India a few months later. Well do we remember how we were awakened twice every night by the voices of the police as they, from the road, called these men by name until they awakened and responded in order to make sure they were not out on some new foraging expedition. The police, not yet realizing what the grace of God could do for such men, did not yet trust them; consequently the men had lived on our mission yard for more than a year before this practice was discontinued.

Twenty years have passed [it is now thirty], but we are happy to tell you that from that time to this there has never been a single criminal record against any of these men. Some have already entered into glory, saved by the blood of the Lamb, and numbered among the children of these converted robbers are some of the finest young workers we have in our mission today.

Kondu's father was one of those criminals. He himself was a boy among those whom A. D. Fritzlan took on the mission compound. On the last Sunday of the camp Kondu told of his experience and exhorted all Christians to have faith in one another like Brother Fritzlan had in those converted criminals.

Paulas Ingle is now a student in our Bible school at Basim, preparing to become a Nazarene preacher. He was until four years ago a sadhu (holy man) of the Hindu faith. He first heard the gospel preached by Sister May Mc-

Kay from the text, "What shall it profit a man, if he shall gain the whole world, and lose his own soul?" Fifteen years later, during the camp in 1947, in which Dr. H. V. Miller was worker, he was saved and sanctified. This year I heard him say: "I attended this camp meeting for many years to see who would profess faith in Christ, so that when they went back to their villages I could seek them out and persuade them to return to Hinduism. But now I am among those who believe in Christ as my Saviour." He now goes to those villages and sings and preaches of His new religion, this great salvation. He has gone back to those people he turned away from Christ and seen every one of them restored to salvation. When he was converted he promised God he would fast every Sunday and pray for those who are still in the darkness. This vow he has kept even when seriously sick in body.

In our last meeting in Buldana, Samuel Bhujbal, district superintendent, excellent interpreter and eloquent preacher, told in his farewell introduction how he was converted. He said in 1921 when he was in school at a distant place someone wrote him a letter to say that a great man from America was coming and asked him to come to the convention to see and hear him. He responded and came to see and hear Dr. H. F. Reynolds. He said, "I was converted then, and soon after right here in this church God sanctified me wholly." When I responded I expressed the hope that my humble ministry of four weeks in India might bear the fruit of at least one outstanding life given to Christ and His service. Today that is my earnest prayer and fond hope. If that is finally accomplished, the trip to India will be rewarded a hundredfold.

Education, the Complement
Of Evangelism

As certain as the evangelist must go before, the teacher must follow after, in successful missionary work. Those missions which have majored on institutional work have inevitably localized their efforts. In many cases they have given the benefits of education and health to those with whom they have labored, without leading them to Christ; or if they have been converted, it was only a formal acceptance of Christianity without supernatural regeneration. On the other hand, those who have engaged in evangelism and have neglected to conduct a program of education have discovered that it was all but impossible to accomplish abiding results. Converts cannot be uprooted from their old religious concepts without being transplanted into the fertile soil of Christian truth. The error and superstition in which they have been bound so long must be replaced by knowledge of the God revealed in Christ, the living Word, and in the Bible, the inscribed Word of God. Their perverted and degraded ideals of conduct must be supplanted by the lofty standards of Christian ethics. Illiteracy, which is never an aid to godliness, must be wiped out where Christ is victorious in the lives of men.

It is not enough to tell people to believe on the Lord Jesus Christ and be saved. They must also be brought into the new life that elevates and uplifts men in body, mind, and spirit. We dare not save people partially; they must be saved wholly. Those who have filthy bodies and homes must be taught cleanliness, hygiene, and sanitation. Those who cannot read and write must be taught enough to help themselves and help others. A few converted in later life may never learn, but their children must be given opportunity for self-improvement. Those who have lived in indolence and poverty must be taught ways and means of gaining a respectable livelihood. Some vocational training is essential.

Failure to meet these elementary and basic demands of a Christian life will mean that those who are converted are in constant danger of reverting to their old ways of life. And their children will be in even greater danger of being absorbed by the spirit of indifference, ignorance, and sin by which they are surrounded. We may for a time carry on with first generation converts; but when their children are old enough to assume the leadership they must be prepared by Christian training to do so, or our immediate success will be hindered and our ultimate defeat assured. Our schools must give us the leaders and workers to carry on as generation after generation passes.

Even the work of evangelism must be done by those who are prepared for it by the processes of Christian education. We can never send enough missionaries to any field to do the work of evangelizing that must be done. The mission must train national pastors and evangelists to do the great bulk of it. This conclusion is inescapable as one reviews the work of our India mission. Even now most of those who are doing effective work have been trained in our schools or were acquired from other missions in the beginning days. A detailed history of our schools in India would make most interesting reading. Such a story would be too long to relate here.

That what our schools have produced is well worth all the money and effort invested in them does not need to be argued. We took a superficial census in the assembly. Of those present, forty-two had attended the Bible school. Most of them were now preachers, teachers, or nurses. An additional sixty-one had attended the other mission schools, either the coeducational school now in operation or the boys' and girls' schools that preceded it. This means that at least half of the entire body of delegates and visitors had been enrolled in the mission schools. The other half of those present were nearly all first generation Nazarenes. Of them there were sixty in number. And there were sixty-five present who had been converted as children less than ten years of age. These figures show conclusively that the future of the mission depends on the effectiveness of its schools. In fact, a study of the records of any missionary undertaking will lead to the same conclusion. The larger success of the whole missionary undertaking must be achieved through the salvation and education of the youth of the nation.

Commendable as the work of our schools has been in the India mission, yet there are some facts that prove that for many years their scope and depth of training was inadequate. It is now forty-five years since the policy was changed to more extensive evangelism after the exodus from Buldana as previously related. But today we have only seven ordained men in the Indian church. Of these, three came to us after they had received their education in other missions. Two received much of their training in the schools of other missions. Only two, therefore, of the seven elders of the present day are the product of our schools. To make that story more impressive, it must be recorded that, although no general superintendent had been in an Indian Assembly for four years, there were no men ready for ordination this year. Of the three recommended, only one received serious consideration by the Board of Orders and Relations. Furthermore, the Board of Ministerial Studies read a report which revealed that those taking the Course of Study had in many instances failed in their examinations. In very recent years the program of education has been much improved. But to fulfill our duty to our future church and its leaders, it must be further strengthened. A plan to offer training in the Bible school that will give adequate educational preparation for ordination is now under consideration and should be put into effect at the earliest possible date. Included in the curriculum should be enough teaching of English to enable workers to read books and periodicals which are not available in Marathi. This is especially needful because the literature for home study simply does not exist. Furthermore, in many instances the homes of national pastors are so modest in space and furnishings that they provide little opportunity for concentrated study.

For the aid of all of our pastors, workers, and laymen a more adequate supply of literature in the Marathi language is an urgent need. At present it is so limited as to be practically nonexistent. Missionary Bronell Greer is making a commendable effort to fill the need by putting out a preachers' magazine on his Marathi typewriter. He is also providing some other articles that are helpful. If one could imagine the church at home without the Nazarene Publishing House and all its productions, he might have some idea of the situation confronting our Indian church. But even then it would not be so bad, for in America there are other sources from which literature of true spiritual value and with clear emphasis on holiness can be obtained. Such sources in India are not in effective operation for holiness groups. The need for translation and publication of literature in India can scarcely be exaggerated. One can hardly conjecture what effect an adequate supply of literature would have upon the progress of our Indian church. Somehow the solution to this problem must be found.

The schools now in operation in India are four in number. Two of them are Bible schools. At Buldana we have the Junior Bible School. Its offerings are for promising laymen. Its purpose is to give them some training, so that they can become effective lay leaders in their local churches. Some of them may receive the call to preach and enter the ministry. It was opened on the advice of Dr. Miller when in India in 1947. This year eight couples and one single man were enrolled. That it will prove a blessing to such as take advantage of it cannot be doubted. The students live on the compound for six months and then return to their home churches for the remainder of the year. The school is under the direction of Brother Weldon Franklin. Practically all the teaching is done by national Christians. Probbaker Bhujbal is the excellent headmaster.

The Senior Bible School is located at Basim. Brother Earl Lee is the missionary in charge. His wife is his able helper. Rev. G. S. Borde, a well-qualified elder, is the headmaster. This year twelve married couples were enrolled. In addition there were five single men. A new building is under construction which will provide living quarters for eight more couples. The enrollment for next year is expected to increase until all available space will be occupied.

The state of the Bible school seemed to be more prosperous and encouraging than ever before. The spirit was excellent. The students are spiritual and they eagerly engage in week-end evangelistic tours. They labored in seventy-eight villages during the last term of school. Their work is effective in the salvation of souls as well as being excellent training for them.

I was honored to be permitted to speak at the graduation exercises this year. One young man and his wife received their diplomas. Last year four were graduated, and a like number are expected to finish the course next year. With the present aggressive leaders permanently assigned to this work the school should grow in numbers and effectiveness. For the present and for the foreseeable future, a strong Bible school that will give full educational qualifications for ordination to its graduates is as far as we need to go in the field of education above the high school level. If college and seminary training are ever undertaken, it will be the result of a more fully developed national church which will demand such advanced training and assume the major portion of the responsibility for supporting such institutions. May God grant that such will be the case if our Lord delays His coming.

There are also two coeducational boarding schools now in successful operation. The school at Dhad is in its first year. It was opened to take the place of two small day schools in remote areas. It is the opinion of our Mission Council that for the present the boarding schools are a better investment than day schools, even for the beginning standards. They believe that by taking the children away from the deplorable home conditions in which they live they can more effectively teach them better standards of living. The school at Dhad serves the children from the newer territory of the district called the Mogalai. It offers instruction in standards 1 to 3. We visited this school just before we left the area for Bombay. The physical equipment is very modest and inexpensive. There is a small compound in the heart of a Hindu-Moslem village. On one side is the humble home of Anand and Leliabai Shinde, the headmaster and his wife. They take all responsibility for administering the school and do all the teaching. Across the courtyard is the school building made of mud walls and a corrugated steel roof. At one end is the kitchen, where a kindly woman of advanced age proudly presides and prepares the simple meals for the seventeen boys and four girls enrolled. Adjoining are the classrooms. They are also used as a dormitory, for at night the children roll out their mats and blankets and sleep there on the *shane* floors. During the day the bedding is neatly packed in small wooden trunks and boxes. In the center of the compound there is a large tree that provides some much-appreciated shade. Beneath it there is a good well that supplies plenty of water.

Shindemaster and Leliabai are doing a wonderful piece of work. Their adviser is Mrs. Ethel Franklin, and no little portion of the credit for the school's initial success belongs to her. She lives eighteen miles away at Buldana and has the responsibility for her home and family there. Besides, she operates the Buldana dispensary and bears many other burdens as missionary in her own right, as well as helping her husband with his varied responsibilities.

The entire school spent the week before our Monday morning visit at the camp meeting. They had returned to the school, twenty-five miles away, in the weapons carrier, arriving about 2:00 a.m. But when we came at ten-thirty everything was in good order around the compound. The children were in favorable contrast to the near-naked, dirty, and unkempt village boys and girls of their age on the streets. Their hair was combed neatly. The boys' pink and green shirts and the girls' blue dresses were clean, and their faces and teeth all looked as if they had been polished. It was thrilling to hear them sing both in English and Marathi, "The B-I-B-L-E," and "He'll Hand Us the Bounty Down." They nearly took the steel roof off the building with their strong, penetrating voices. Then there was a special by four boys and one girl. It was a temperance song. Each one sang one of the following verses:

Elephants don't drink; why should I?
Dogs don't drink; why should I?
Birds don't drink; why should I?
Tigers don't drink; why should I?
Cows don't drink; why should I?

There was a refrain after each verse in which all joined in a temperance pledge. Then the headmaster sang a psalm, and after each verse they answered antiphonally.

There was also a testimony meeting. They gave good evidence of having been to camp meeting. Some testified they had been saved at camp; one had been sanctified too. Others had received new strength to live for Christ. One had been kept well even if a scorpion had bitten him. Needless to say, we left the school fully persuaded that the investment there will pay big dividends in years to come.

But the most inspiring feature of the entire mission program is the coeducational boarding school at Chikhli. It was decided to try the experiment in 1944. Then only the first standards from the boys' and girls' schools were brought together. By 1946 the amalgamation was completed, and now courses are offered in standards 1 to 9, with full recognition by the Indian government. The time may come when the demand will be made for the inclusion of two more standards, which would be sufficient to complete high school training.

Unstinted praise goes to Mrs. Orpha Cook, now on furlough, for the outstanding success of this undertaking. To be sure, there were many difficulties to be overcome, and sometimes the discouragements yet seem so many and great that those who bear the burden are tempted to think it is too much. But then they see what is being done for the youth of our Indian church and remember that in a few years those boys and girls will be the Christian leaders of the church and their communities, and they take heart. At present Rev. Leslie Fritzlan is in charge of the school, besides serving as chairman of the Mission Council. His wife ably assists him in this great work. All of the teaching is done by nationals. Most of them have been converted and received their elementary education in the mission schools. The headmaster is John Meshramker, a fine, capable Christian of excellent ability and spirit. We were pleased to see the boys and girls at play. On separate courts they were at games of volley-ball. This not only provides exercise for the building of strong, well bodies, but also teaches them the give-and-take lessons they need so much to learn. They also learn to play the game fairly and according to the rules. They find that they can lose gracefully and win humbly. But more important, they learn in a coeducational school to give proper respect to those of the opposite sex. In a land where unquestioned superiority has been accorded to the males of the species without regard to moral character or intellectual capacity, *this is important.* It will not only work for the emancipation of Christian womanhood, but will also prove beneficial to men.

It was interesting to see them at their meals. They are given abundance of clean, healthful food. It is cooked for the boys by Indian women according to their customs and tastes. The girls cook and serve their own meals. When the time comes to eat, the boys sit in long lines on the gravel-covered ground of the compound. Copious portions of rice and curry were served to all. Then with good etiquette, according to Indian standards, they ate it with their fingers. They are so skilled in doing it that it did not seem at all uncouth. They take turns in serving. Each one waits until all have been served, including those who have done the work. God's blessing is invoked upon their meal.

But our most thrilling experience came when we visited the entire school, including all the teachers and pupils, in the chapel. There the boys sat on the floor on one side. The girls were on the other side. There are 142 boys in the boarding school and 120 girls. Besides, there are about 25 who live in their nearby homes. Thus the total enrollment is about 285. In the chapel service an excellent program of songs and readings was presented. It was especially encouraging to observe the girls participate with freedom. Some seem to have really found deliverance from their timidity and inhibition. The entire program was carried forward with commendable ease and efficiency. We were given an enthusiastic welcome and a cordial response to our remarks.

After the chapel service we went out to the new building, which provides some administrative offices and several classrooms. Rev. Ralph Cook had seen the building well on its way to completion before leaving on furlough. There was a brief dedication service, in which we were honored to participate.

As we left those meetings that day we felt fully convinced that the future success of our work in India is assured if we can only train the boys and girls under Christian influence and see them established in vital experiences of saving and sanctifying grace. Our task in education will in large measure be in training the product of our Christian homes. Some from Hindu and Moslem families may attend the schools and be won for Christ, but the schools are a necessity for saving our own youth. And they will be the means for preparing pastors, evangelists, and teachers to reach the masses of India. Yes, Christian education is a part of the work of evangelism. It conserves the fruit and prepares the future leaders. For every argument we can produce for Christian schools in America, we can produce one far more weighty for them in India.

These prepared young men will be the pastors and leaders of our churches, and their prepared wives can help them sponsor elementary schools in connection with their churches until in every Christian community the curse of illiteracy will be wiped out. Herein lies the hope of our mission and the hope of India.

The Case for Medical Missions

For forty-five years our Nazarene mission in India has carried on in harmony with its policy as stated in these words, "Evangelism, first and chief, with institutions second and auxiliary—the one the legitimate outgrowth of the other." The work of evangelism is being pushed with unabated zeal in ever-increasing thoroughness and in an ever-growing area. And now the educational work is fitting into the pattern as a normal complement of the work of evangelism. The third phase of the program, namely, medical missions, has also been gradually growing in its importance and scope until today it is no longer incidentally included in the plans for the present and future, but is in fact another major consideration in the development of the Church of the Nazarene in India.

Many missionaries with no special training in the field of medicine have done much to relieve the suffering of the people among whom they have labored. Seeing the need, they have acquired books on medicine, equipped themselves with medical kits, and have gone about their work dealing out simple cures to the people. Many have carried forceps to pull aching teeth. They have washed out infected wounds, poured in disinfectants, and bound them up with a prayer that their not too skillful efforts might prove effective. Doubtless their prayers were a big factor in the success of their administrations of medicine. While such work is good, it is perfectly obvious that it is inadequate to meet the needs of a great and growing missionary enterprise.

The next step in medical missions in India as well as in many other fields has been the sending of well-trained nurses to open and operate dispensaries and carry on the work as far as their skill and training would justify. These, too, have often gone far beyond what they would be expected or allowed to do in the homeland. With daring and with great faith in God they have done their best and they have been a great blessing to the people. But such a ministry does not lessen the demand for doctors and a hospital; it rather heightens the demand and accentuates the need, for there is so much that must be done and the ability to do is not possessed. Therefore, the demand for doctors and a hospital is ever more urgent.

One of the insistent demands arises from the need of proper medical care for the missionaries and their families. This is especially urgent in a country like India, where deadly disease germs fill the dust-laden air in the dry season and infest the whole environment in every season. Missionaries must always trust God for the preservation of their health and for healing when they are sick. Some remarkable instances of healing have been witnessed among our missionaries in India. Notably there was the miraculous restoration of Brother Tracy when national doctors and all attending him saw no hope whatever of his recovery from typhoid fever. The effect of his healing had very beneficial influence upon the missionaries and the national people who observed it. But though he was healed, several have died on the field. Some of them might have been spared had up-to-date medical care been available. Many others have been forced to leave the field because of ill health. Some of them could probably have stayed if the proper health aids had been within their reach.

The program for expansion in India calls for thirty missionaries on the staff. Five or six of them should normally be on furlough each year. With twenty-four or twenty-five on the field, with children being born and reared there in increasing numbers, the need of doctors, nurses, and a hospital is evident.

There is another mission board operating in adjacent territory to our India district. When they began years ago, the board and the entire church were strongly committed to healing of the body in answer to the prayer of faith. Therefore, being consistent with their teachings, they had no thought for medical missions at all. Those ideas have been modified somewhat and they have even sent forth a doctor to one of their fields. In India they are with increasing frequency calling upon our Nazarene doctors for medical attention, which, to be sure, is gladly given. Recently Dr. Witthoff gave eight of their missionaries help in one day. There is yet another mission nearby which is glad to use the facilities made available by our medical program. They are grateful for the service and ready to pay for it. We are, in turn, happy to be of all possible aid to those who with us seek to save India's millions. It all goes to show that medical missions is a boon to the missionaries and their families.

This need has long been keenly felt by missionaries. For twelve months Henry Martyn, the first Protestant missionary to Near East countries, spent his waning strength in translating the New Testament and Psalms into the Persian language. After finishing that stupendous undertaking, and realizing that his strength was fast failing, he started on a 1,500-mile trek on horseback to Constantinople, en route to England. He did not reach his immediate destination. He died on October 16, 1812, at the early age of thirty-one. Seven years later Pliny Fisk and Levi Parsons were sent out from America to carry the gospel to the land where Christ was born. In three years Levi Parsons died in Alexandria, Egypt. Pliny Fisk wrote home to the American board citing the need for medical missionaries. Two years later, when he himself was stricken with fever, he wrote again to his board as follows.

> I felt more than I ever felt before the need of a skillful and faithful physician. We had no medical adviser in whom we could repose the least confidence. Our chest of medicines, one or two medical books, and our very limited experience were all we had to depend upon. It is quite probable that proper treatment might have removed the fever at once. As it lingered, we often doubted what course to pursue. . . . . May we not hope that the churches of our Lord which have sent us to this land will ere long send to our aid a skillful physician who will watch over our bodily health and also assist us in our spiritual labors.

His appeal brought results.

It is sometimes suggested that there are national doctors and hospitals available. This is true, but in India and many other countries these are not as yet reliable for serious ailments. Several of them operate in the larger towns in our district. While we were in India at the camp meeting, word reached us that a little boy had died at the hospital in Buldana. He had been sick for some time. The national doctor at the hospital diagnosed his ailment as malaria and treated him accordingly. A few hours before the child died he changed his diagnosis to typhoid fever and pneumonia. It was too late now to save the little fellow's life. Probably his ailment was typhoid all along, and when the pneumonia set in he was too weak to resist both of those dread diseases. Such a thing could happen to a missionary's child or to the missionary himself. .

It was a comfort to us to see a neat unit built alongside the Reynolds Memorial Hospital for the special use of sick missionaries and their families. During the year past it had been in frequent use, and without it the lives of the missionaries or their children would have been in grave danger. Their appreciation for the hospital and medical staff may be understood more fully after reading the following quotation from Brother Beals's report to the Council in 1947:

My recent prolonged illness with diphtheria, my first serious illness for twelve years, was a time of trial, but withal a time of blessing and rest as well. I am deeply indebted to Dr. Orpha Speicher and also to Miss Chappell and Miss Darling, our nurses, who cared for me during this time. I could not have had better care.

Only those who have been, as I have been, in other hospitals in India can fully appreciate what it meant to be in our own Nazarene Hospital and in the hands of our own Nazarene staff during an illness like this. May God bless them.

The appalling need of India's disease-ridden masses is, however, the greater argument for medical missions. It is obvious that nurses, doctors, dispensaries, and hospitals can never take the place of personal hygiene, public sanitation, and proper nutrition. But these things will never be known among a people where the ministry of health according to enlightened standards is absent. One can see as he passes people on the streets and highways that their need is desperate. Eyes are blind either partially or totally in many instances; teeth are gone or in terrible condition; skin diseases are all but universal. Dr. Witthoff told us of people coming to the hospital with flesh wounds full of maggots. Burns are common among women and children. There were two cases of serious burns brought to the hospital while we were in Basim a few days. Both of them had been treated by plastering the injured skin with tar. During one day forty women came to seek treatment and cure for their sterility at one of the dispensaries visited each month by Dr. Witthoff. Thirty-two of them were barren because of venereal diseases. This is but a suggestion of the extent of such diseases in India. Besides, there are the ever-recurring instances of the plague, smallpox, typhoid fever, diphtheria, cholera, pneumonia, and countless others.

A recent experience since our return to the United States is further proof that medical work is an important and needed phase of the missionary undertaking. Rats began dying on the hospital and Bible school compounds at Basim. Upon examination it was found that they were infected with the dread bubonic plague. With speedy decision and action Dr. Evelyn Witthoff ordered poison distributed in proper places. At the same time she imposed every known precaution upon all human residents of the area. Dead rats were then found in increasing numbers. Now it was necessary to make post-mortem examination of every carcass to determine whether the victim had died of the poison or the plague.

It was time for the annual meeting of the Mission Council at Chikhli sixty miles away. The missionaries gathered from their various stations. They went to prayer to intercede for an intervention of divine providence. Chairman Leslie Fritzlan cabled the office of foreign missions in Kansas City. He did not conceal the gravity of the situation in Basim. He reported as follows: "Rats are dying of bubonic plague on the hospital and Bible school compounds. It is a miracle that so far there have been no cases among human beings. Dr. Witthoff and Nurse Chappell have remained at their posts of duty to do everything possible to stay the plague. Please request prayer by the church in this grave crisis."

The news spread rapidly. Many importunate and impassioned prayers were offered.

God heard and answered prayer. The plague was stayed! But who can doubt that the courageous fight waged by those medical missionaries was the instrument in God's hands by which the tragedy was averted? While others prayed, they prayed and worked with all their skill and strength. Their frail lives stood between life and death. But for them the Christian community of Basim might have been wiped out. The deadly plague could have raged on until thousands and tens of thousands of human lives were lost.

Of course, we can adopt the attitude held and advocated by those of pagan mind that life is cheap, that human bodies and personalities are not sacred, and that the law of the survival of the fittest should be allowed to operate unhindered in order to keep the population from becoming excessive and burdensome. No one who seeks to follow the footsteps of the Great Physician can hold such views. Even a humanitarian philosophy of life, to say nothing of the Christian concept of the dignity and value of the human personality, will rule out such low and degraded opinions. To accept those dogmas would mean that we would soon forfeit the distinctive virtues of our Christian faith. We would be converts to Hinduism rather than making converts to Christ. Our responsibility to minister health to the bodies as well as salvation to the souls of men is inescapable in the light of our Christian understanding of life.

The lifting of this dread burden of disease and death from the two millions of people in our territory in India by our modest efforts in medical missions is clearly out of the question. But we are beginning a work which will go on and on through those whose lives are changed by the power of God. Among the people there are nurses and doctors of their own nationality who have received their inspiration and their training, in part, at the Nazarene Hospital and School of Nursing. This good hope is already beginning to bear fruit. We saw three young women graduated from the Nurses' Training Course this year. Mrs. Williamson addressed them at their graduation. This number will increase until there will be a nurse in every village or nearby. One of these was a preacher's wife, who also graduated with him from the Bible school. With poise and confidence she will teach the people of the churches they serve the way of life for their souls and the way of health for their bodies. She is the first of many, we trust, who will be prepared for such a service to the people of India. Already these nurses graduated or in training are bearing a major share of the burden of the nursing at the hospital. They even give all injections except intravenously.

Unless we undertake the missionary task with the determination to do our work with depth and systematic thoroughness, we will be in danger of consenting to be as superficial and inadequate as the Indian farmers are in the cultivation of the soil. With no fertilizer, no crop rotation, no improved means or methods, they go on scratching the surface of the ground and gathering only a small per cent of the harvest which the soil is capable of yielding. To do our work adequately, we must see men's lives changed and redeemed, body, mind, and soul.

Medical missions will, in the long run, prove to be a powerful ally to the work of evangelism. By such means, many hearts have already been opened to light and truth in India. Some direct results have been gained. One evening the missionaries at Basim were together for a time of fellowship. We noticed that Dr. Witthoff disappeared. After an hour she came in again. When asked what had happened, with her characteristic modesty she told how a patient had been brought to the hospital who, in her judgment, was "demon possessed." Later we learned that the woman had been so violent that it took four men to hold her. In their desperation they had even stood on her body. But when the Basim missionaries came to camp meeting a week later, they were telling with great joy how that woman had been led to call on Christ for deliverance, and that when she prayed in His almighty name the demons left her. Thereafter she was "clothed" and in her "right mind." Yes, the doctors and the nurses are soul-winning evangelists too, and they open to the gospel many hearts and homes which will eventually receive the Christ that saves from all sin.

The question of how widely and how rapidly our efforts should be extended is certain to be raised. That we are to keep on pushing back the frontiers is not the point; of that we have no doubt. But while we are ever enlarging our borders, we must also finish the work already begun. We could spread ourselves so thin that we would do nothing thoroughly. We ought to remember that there are two methods of expansion. One is by establishing a new base of operations; the other is by fanning out from a base already established. Sometimes we need to do both. At present it seems apparent that we can win more souls by operating from our present installations than by opening in new territory. In India we have now two million people in the field which is assigned exclusively to us. Of that number, two thousand have been effectively reached for Christ. This means that one out of one thousand has been baptized. There is yet much to do in our present district. Some of our converts have been forced to move to cities like Nagpur and Bombay. They are eager to start churches in those cities, which are open to evangelization by all groups. To do so would be a wise procedure, both to conserve the fruit of our labors and extend our influence for Christ. This can be done from our present base.

The union of several holiness bodies in the Church of the Nazarene found us with three different fields in India. The churches of the East, as we have already noted, were sponsoring the work centered in Buldana, Berar. The Pentecostal Mission of Nashville, Tennessee, under the leadership of Rev. J. O. McClurkan, united with the Church of the Nazarene in 1915. This resulted in a "fusion" of the work they had promoted in the Thana District near Bombay with the work in Berar. The Thana District was, however, administered in connection with the work in Berar until 1931. The church in the West had opened work in eastern India. This, too, was maintained until 1931. At that time Dr. J. W. Goodwin and Dr. R. T. Williams visited the three areas and, after carefully reviewing the situation, they made their historic recommendation that the work in eastern India be closed and that the missionaries and workers in the Thana District near Bombay be moved and co-ordinated with the mission in Berar. This recommendation was adopted and put into effect. The Berar field has been enlarged in several expansive measures, but we operate from one base, under one leadership, and in an area where one language is spoken.

The decision made back in 1931 was the cause of some real heartaches, and perhaps a few were never quite reconciled to it, but time has proved it was wise. In crisic times the missionary staff has been reduced to four; but with the work all within range of their supervision, even under those conditions it has moved forward. And now if conditions in India and the world remain settled, we can do our work both extensively and intensively. In other words, we will be able to do the work of evangelizing and at the same time we will have the personnel and resources to do the educational and medical work so badly needed to fully develop our field.

It does not seem illogical to conclude that these facts might give us some guidance in our policy of expansion for the future. Let us reach everyone possible with the gospel, but let us also work the fields we have opened with sufficient thoroughness to gather a bountiful harvest rather than a meager one. Our field in India is producing thirty and sixty fold. We can make it yield a hundredfold with God's blessing.

Dr. Orpha Speicher was the first Nazarene doctor to be appointed to India. She reached the field in 1936. No doubt her name will live long among the Indian Christians and the lovers of the missionary cause in America for what she has done in pioneering the Nazarene medical work in India. She had only the equipment she had brought with her, and that was not very extensive for opening a hospital.

The building had been used as a boys' school by the Methodist mission, which sold many of the buildings we now own in Basim to us in 1935. As a young missionary, Dr. Speicher must have received most of her inspiration from the fact she was answering God's call to minister health and salvation to the needy people of India. With courage she tackled her problems. Under her supervision a veranda was built along the front of the long, low building. The rooms were adapted as best they could be to offices for admissions, records, and examinations. The other rooms were equipped with beds of the Indian variety. During her second term on the field, Dr. Speicher had the satisfaction of seeing a beautiful little chapel erected, adjoining the old building; and just before she left for her second furlough, the surgical building was completed and put into use. This gave some needed space for more beds in the old unit. Two other additions are now under construction. When they are finished the hospital for women and children will be quite adequate. Gradually items of equipment have been acquired. There is still a wide margin between what is available in that hospital and the up-to-date institutions which we see in the United States, but much progress has been made.

Now the entire Mission Council is enthusiastically eager for the appointment of a male doctor. Unconverted Indian men will not accept treatment at the hands of a woman doctor; neither will women readily consult a male doctor. To serve the purposes of a hospital with the greatest success, both are needed. Dr. Witthoff and Dr. Speicher join in the petition that a male doctor be sent to aid them as soon as possible. This will require a moderate outlay of money for a new unit to house the men patients. The few who come now occupy places on beds or on the floor of the veranda. In spite of their limitations, the doctors and nurses in the hospital and dispensaries treated 12,000 patients and collected $5,421 in fees last year. With the addition of the men's unit and a male doctor, the number of patients as well as income would be greatly increased.

Another imperative in equipment is an X ray. The new surgical unit can be used for both men and women. To keep an adequate staff of doctors it will be necessary to have at least three on the field. One of them would, of course, be on furlough at least half of the time. Dr. Witthoff loves the work of traveling to the villages to visit the dispensaries. She would gladly move her residence to Chikhli, where she could serve as doctor for the co-educational school and work out from there in the dispensaries.

Both Dr. Speicher and Dr. Witthoff are splendid examples in spirit and in ability. If we are to send the ever-increasing number of young men and young women who feel called to be medical missionaries to the field, they must follow the pattern set by these consecrated women doctors. We cannot hope to provide great modern buildings and all the up-to-date equipment that surgeons could use, for years to come. The missionary doctor must be ready to accept handicaps and hardships. For the sake of Christ and the suffering humanity He lived and died to save, they must go forth to work in His vineyard with such tools as may be available, and live in the hope that eventually a larger, better day will come.

* * * *

This chapter was largely written on board ship only a few days after leaving India. Upon our arrival at home two months later, we found Dr. A. Milton Smith and Kansas City First Church eager to undertake the raising of money to build a men's unit for the hospital in Basim and a home for the missionary doctor. In one service they pledged $12,000 to be paid in one year. This is above their general budget, which is now $11,000 per year. The official board of the church has voted to make it at least $15,000.

The General Board has already placed Dr. and Mrs. Ira Cox under appointment. They expect to reach India in the autumn of 1952. By the time they have completed language study the new buildings will be ready for them.

They Speak for Themselves

The missionaries in India have a custom which they have observed for years. They meet together one day in each month for prayer. On this particular field, they are fortunate in that they live close enough to one another so that, by arranging a central place, all are able to come. However, this is not without some personal inconvenience and sacrifice. In the days of petrol rationing (which has recently been removed), it took some planning. Mothers with small children must provide for their care. Busy nurses and doctors and evangelists and teachers must all make special arrangements to leave their stations even for a few hours. But I heard them say repeatedly, "We will give up anything before we give up our day of prayer."

They have the understanding that each missionary in the group may pray until he is fully satisfied. There are no time limits. Burdens and problems are thus shared. Weary, tense bodies relax under the combined weight of unified petition. Sorrows and cares slip away as the sympathetic understanding of others reveals anew the Master's unfailing sympathy and His undying love. No wounded feelings toward a brother or sister missionary can be cherished when one hears him cry out his heart to God in earnest, heartfelt prayer. From the first we marveled at the gracious spirit of perfect accord that seemed to be theirs. Strong-minded men and women of diverse temperament and training are blended here into a smoothly functioning organism. They maintain that their prayer day is the answer. Not once in four weeks among them did we hear one speak in any way disparagingly of another. Unity, respect, love, tolerance, and self-effacement characterize the group. Wonderful is the power of prayer! When all hearts are satisfied and all minds are clear they break bread together, transact any necessary business, and depart for their individual stations fortified by their common vision and faith for another arduous period of labor.

With this background it is evident that all anticipated the Council meeting at Basim with keen delight. Under Hazel Lee's excellent supervision, everyone ate together at one long table in her dining room. From the first meal fun was in order; but no matter whom the laugh was on, he or she took it in good part, being assured that before the day was over the tables would be turned.

There were preaching services morning and evening with only the missionaries present. As Mr. Williamson brought the living Word, we feasted together and renewed our spiritual strength.

The reports of the missionaries were rich beyond words to describe. As these noble soldiers modestly recounted battles fought and victories won, all eyes were bathed in tears, and time and again there was pause for prayer or for praise to God. The printed page will not reveal the warm color of the voice nor the glory upon the face as these accounts were read. But no record of this visit to India would be complete without a word from the missionaries themselves. Consequently these paragraphs have been lifted out of their written reports and are herewith presented.

Leslie C. Fritzlan, Missionary Chairman

The spirit of co-operation and dedication and the sustained note of faith and expectancy to be found in this missionary group in India have never failed to warm my own heart and I would rather be a member of this fellowship than any other I know on earth.

Concerning church statistics, the figures we have for the year ending last March show a total of 1,213 full members of the church and 484 probationers. Thirty new members were received by baptism, that is, conversion from Hinduism.

Over the district the 22 churches, the 22 Church Missionary Societies, 9 Nazarene Young People's Societies, and the Sunday schools gave a total of Rs. 8,600. There were 149 Sunday schools with a total enrollment of 3,895 and average attendance of 2,900.

Considering the hopeless pace of building work in rural India it can be said that much indeed was accomplished along this line: a beautiful chapel and surgery for the hospital, a fine auto-clave to replace open charcoal braziers, and the foundations for maternity and surgical wards; the handsome Dittmore Memorial Bible School Chapel at Basim in which we are now assembled and extra classrooms from the former chapel; the completion of the comfortable bungalow at Chikhli, now occupied by the Bealses; a most useful windmill and the completion of the new administration building with four large classrooms and offices at the Chikhli School; a spacious church in Mehkar with dispensary facilities adjoining— this the reward of much faith and perseverance in the face of baffling red tape lasting years; a good site at Parad for a U.S. Servicemen's Memorial Chapel at Anwa; property in four towns in the territory recently acquired from the Church of Scotland Mission in the southwest part of the district; a new servants' unit in Buldana to replace what were becoming hovels.

I thank God for the high privilege of serving Him in this needy land; for good health; for the indispensable, glad help of my wife in so many things; for the fine fellowship of our whole missionary family, sustained through work, problems and committees and deepened by monthly days of prayer and praise together; for our Indian brethren and the Church, whose real interests we are here to serve; and above all for the present knowledge of sins forgiven and a heart cleansed from all sin through the precious blood of the Son of God.

Mrs. Leslie Fritzlan

Keeping accounts, writing letters, disciplining school children, assisting the I.D.A. treasurer in a small measure, auditing mission accounts, packing suitcases and bedrolls for a frequently-traveling husband—these all are a part of the necessary but less-inspiring side of life.

In all things God has blessed and taught me new lessons. Often I feel very slow to learn and yet He is so patient. I praise Him for the certainty of sins forgiven and the joy of the Holy Spirit abiding within.

Just before moving to Chikhli the following poem by Annie Johnson Flint* came in a letter from a friend, just when I most needed it. It is my testimony today.

He giveth more grace when the burdens grow greater;
   He sendeth more strength when the labors increase;
To added affliction He addeth His mercy;
   To multiplied trials He multiplies peace.

When we have exhausted our store of endurance,
   When our strength has failed ere the day is half done,
When we reach the end of our hoarded resources—
   Our Father's full giving is only begun.

His love has no limit, His grace has no measure,
   His power no boundary known unto men,
For out of His infinite riches in Jesus
   He giveth and giveth and giveth again.

* Copyright, Reprinted by permission.
Evangelical Publishers, Toronto 1, Canada

Prescott L. Beals

Personally I praise God that the same Saviour who sent us out to India many years ago is still my very own personal Saviour. And the same Holy Spirit who came down in sanctifying, glorious power in that mighty Northwest Nazarene College Pentecost thirty-three years ago still abides today. Hallelujah to the Lamb forever! Glory!

It was hard to leave our boys so far away. The first Sunday at sea, after waving our final farewells to them that same morning as they stood on the Golden Gate Bridge, I had the greatest test of my consecration I ever had in my life. But we are here in India, we believe, in God's order; and such being the case, we can and do leave our precious boys in the hands of our Lord and Saviour.

There is just one real reason why we have left them and returned to India. And that is that, under the blessing of God, it may be possible for us to have a share in helping the Indian church to have some more mighty outpourings of the Holy Spirit. Oh, for a mighty Holy Ghost revival in every one of our churches throughout our district! Brethren, we must have this at all costs. "Holiness, holiness, holiness" must be our watchword and cry. For with our churches set on fire the flames will spread until, with India as hungry as she is, and with the doors open in India as they have never been before, thousands shall fall at the feet of our Saviour, and confess Him as their Lord and King. Impossible? No! Not with God still on the throne. Hallelujah!

Thanks to my good wife, who has stood by me through the years, and who has been ready to return to India too. And thanks to our chairman, Leslie Fritzlan, who is almost like a son or younger brother to me, and to his good wife, and to all the others. Brethren, pray for us. And God bless you all!

Mrs. P. L. Beals

The cost to us in coming to India this time, leaving aged parents and our two sons, was the greatest it has ever been. [Since this was written, Mrs. Beals has lost her mother in July, '51.] But I love God with my whole heart and, after "being all for God" for forty years, I am too old "in the Way" to start saying, "The price is too great." I am glad to be in India and I want most of all that the closing years of service count for the Kingdom.

My work is that of being an accompanist rather than a soloist. It has been a thrill these past four months visiting the district churches with my husband even though part of my time is taken up with tiffin baskets, coffeepot, and bedrolls. On these tours in care of the churches, it is a joy, after looking back on thirty years of work, prayers and tears, to look up our children and our grandchildren in the Lord, as we now have third generation Christians. It is a joy to sort over hand-picked fruit. Some may not shine so much yet, but no diamond shines when first mined, not until it is cut and polished.

The Council selected me as treasurer for the mission last September. There is satisfaction in this work, for when red lines are drawn for a balance, then I know that I am right in something. There is joy in the work until ten o'clock at night, after that it is drudgery.

I love God with my whole heart. It is wonderful to serve our church in India.

Mrs. Ruby Blackman

At the last annual Council meeting I was appointed to assist with the work in the N.C.C. School in Chikhli, taking care of the medical work, and evangelistic work. Needless to say, I have found plenty to keep me busy. Work with young people is always interesting and, I feel, most profitable.

Many of them come from "jungly" homes, dirty and unkempt; but after a few months in our care, under Christian influence a marked change takes place, slowly of course but surely. The darkness of heathenism gradually disappears and the beautiful light of the gospel shines forth.

In addition to my medical work at the Chikhli School where I find supreme happiness ministering to the bodies and souls of the children, with Rev. Salve, my Bible woman, and sometimes others I have visited some thirty-one nearby villages. We leave at the early break of day and try to reach the village before the people leave for their day's work out in the fields. As we find a place to hold the service, at once the people gather and listen with real interest to all that is said. When we look upon the multitudes of people all about us, see the darkness of their hearts and minds, the surroundings in which they live, the dirt and filth everywhere, we are inclined to feel the hopelessness of the great task which we try to do. Then when we return to our stations and see the happy faces of those God has given, we are seized with new courage. Out there in the village it's darkness and heathenism, but here it is light and happiness. I never look into the faces of those whom God has redeemed without a deep feeling of praise and thanksgiving for every one He has given us.

Ralph A. Cook

The work of the Chikhli District, which has been our main task for the year, has gone along well.

We have also been busy with our share of building work. The evangelistic bungalow is now completed. The administration building at the coeducational school at Chikhli has been roofed and the main unit completed. The main bungalow at Chikhli and school compound have been fenced with barbed wire.

To come to the end of a term of service and look forward to furloughing home is always difficult. We would praise Him for each missionary and Indian colaborer and we believe that we have the finest group in any mission anywhere on the earth. We want to thank each of you with whom we have labored for your prayers, your patience, your long-suffering, and your love. And now, "Finally, brethren, farewell. Be perfect, be of good comfort, be of one mind, live in peace; and the God of love and peace shall be with you" (II Cor. 13:11).

Orpha Cook

It has been a privilege to serve at our District School. Our aim has been to build Christian character. I have had many opportunities to deal with our boys and girls personally and I believe we have some good leaders in our present student body. Frequently some boy or girl who has a personal problem comes in to "talk it over" and pray their way through in my office.

Our enrollment at the Nazarene Coeducational Christian School for this year is 285.

At present we have Standards I through IX and a teaching staff of ten full-time and four part-time teachers. The District Inspector of Schools, after thoroughly inspecting our school, has recommended us for permanent recognition.

For the year we have taken in Rs. 4,468-03-0 in fees. This amount does not include the wood, chicken, *dhal*, peppers, brooms, hay, eggs, and vegetables taken in as fees. On registration day we took in 60 chickens on back fees.

We have 45 freeship holders. Special work is given to these students so that they may, to some extent, feel that they are working their way through school.

The never ending correspondence and office work always challenges one and I find it takes a good share of my time.

The greatest privilege of all is that of serving our Master and working in His vineyard. I wish to express my appreciation of our missionary group. It has been an honor to work with you and I feel you are more closely related to me than my blood relations. I pray that while we are in America we may continue to serve India and that our future may be ordered of the Lord.

G. Weldon Franklin

The Church of Jesus Christ has aptly been referred to as the Ship of Zion. If we think of her as the flagship of a fleet of ships bound for the heavenly port, then I think it will be permissible to refer to Buldana district and the work in the area as the good steamship "Buldana." She has weathered many a storm, been battered by many a high sea and, except for some needed paint and touch-ups, she still rates as seaworthy. However, the crew and officers of the vessel for some time have been asking the Captain to bring her to dry dock for a major overhaul and renovation. There are compass and barometer readings (the pressure is on the increase) which indicate this prayer will be answered during this Mid-Century Crusade. When this time comes the land-lubbers will put it this way—"A revival has struck old Buldana!"

Jesus, the Commander in Chief of the whole spiritual warfare, is, in a very personal way, the Captain of our ship. There is no better one to be had! What could I say to add to His name except to mention that He has won the full loyalty of every true officer and crewman on board.

In the seas which our ship patrols there are three worldly gathering places called *yatrs*—a county fair and a heathen camp meeting all rolled into one. In each place we have attempted to introduce our Captain and sell as many as possible of the story of His life written up by the four well-known skippers—Matthew, Mark, Luke, and John. Some lines were drawn in these campaigns which helped to remove in people's minds the twilight zone which has existed between right and wrong, between being nominally Christian and truly Christian. Some stowaways were discovered. Among the number several decided to become true crew members. However, others eluded the searching process and are still stowaways. What frightens and burdens me is that these are liable to get caught in the bilge pump and discarded and so miss the battle or even passage altogether. This is the place to pray!

Ethel Franklin

On October 20, I assumed responsibility for the Dhad Primary Boarding School. As Dhad is eighteen miles away from our home, transportation is not always easy—especially if our station wagon has a broken spring. But God has wonderfully blessed. In December we had a revival in the school with Probbaker Bhujbal as evangelist. His last service was a never-to-be-forgotten one. Each child was to bring one thorn to represent each sin he had committed. Some brought seven or eight thorns. Each came forward and named the sins as he threw his thorns into an iron basket. The preacher then burned them as the children prayed for forgiveness. Although there are many obstacles in the way, still God is blessing this school.

Being a mother to our two children, Paul and Judy, has taken no little part of my time, and I would have it no other way. Filling in for Weldon when he is gone, whether in building supervision or accounts or just listening to people's troubles and stories, keeps me doing things I never dreamed I would ever be able to do. The Lord has taught me that the many who come to our compound are just as needy as those who stay at home. So I have begun a special ministry of witnessing to almost every one who comes. I praise my Saviour for the souls who have been saved this year because of our women's prayer meetings; one just went out into eternity. Most of all I praise Him for His presence in my heart and life. I could not do without Him for one single day. Praise His name!

Clarence L. Carter

This moment finds me joyful in heart and grateful to God for what He has done for me. He forgave me my sins one wonderful day, and for Jesus sake sanctified my soul. While I was in school at Nampa, God broke my heart with the needs of India, and I have earnestly sought to do His will ever since. To top it all off, as we knelt in the Mehkar bungalow on our first day of prayer, God spoke again to my heart to let me know that all is well with my soul, and today I have the blessed assurance of being in the will of God.

It has been my privilege to preach five times since arriving in India last September, twice in the local churches, and three times in villages. I was especially moved when over 100 villagers sat in the chilly air around my jeep one night, and after the message they all raised their hands requesting prayer and by that indicated that they would like to have the eternal life which is in Christ Jesus.

And now, while waiting for the opening of language school in Mahableshwar, I enjoy being Brother Franklin's mechanical assistant to overhaul jeeps.

Marjorie Carter

The sea was beautiful as we were coming up along the coast of India. There was a rainbow in every wave, reminding us that God's promises are true even in India.

It was four months ago that we arrived in Bombay. There has been no feeling of strangeness as one would expect in a foreign land, but just a kind of "at home" feeling. How glad we were to see the missionaries, and how we do appreciate the hospitality of the Franklins and their help as well as that of the other missionaries in becoming adjusted here! It was with a bit of fear and trembling that we ventured into our own home with what looked to me like very complicated housekeeping, within such a few days of the time of our arrival. It has been wonderful and I am thankful for the experience it has given me. Home has never meant so much to me as it has in India. For a few weeks we studied under the instruction of a pundit. I have found language study to be a thrilling experience and have felt the very definite help of the Lord. Hearing so much Marathi that I do not understand is the greatest trial I have had and I intend that that shall soon be past. The Holy Spirit abides in my heart today. How grateful I am for the comfort, joy, and strength that come from His presence!

J. W. Anderson

The Lord has given us a good year in Mehkar Circle. We have five organized churches with 125 members and probationers. During the last fiscal year Rs. 667-5-0 was given for all purposes. One new outstation was opened at Kwali with good prospects. An inquirers' meeting was held during the year on the Lonar road with the assistance of Rev. S. J. Bhujbal. At this meeting 30 people were in attendance, 15 were baptized, and 6 children were dedicated. In all since last November we have 25 baptisms on Mehkar District.

We now look forward to the time when we shall proceed to America on furlough. We thank God for His grace and help during this term of service. He has richly blessed us with good health, wonderful fellowship with our fellow missionaries and Indian colaborers and His love, which has been unfailing. I love Him today and want His will for my life.

Mary Anderson

Preached 43 times
Actively assisted in 22 other services
Visited 31 villages in Mehkar Circle
Visited Mehkar village 77 times
Treatments given in small dispensary, 847
Homes visited, 1,003
Meals served to guests in our home, 1,624
Books read, 97
Read the Bible through 3 times
Letters written, 2,628
Travel by train 3,000 miles, by car 2,418, by bus 162, by cart 81, and walked 308 miles

Agnes Willox

Statistics for the Dispensary at Pusad
September, 1949—April, 1950

Number treated in dispensary	1,945
Visited in homes	285
Treated in other villages	100
Midwifery cases	8
Inoculations	100
Total	2,438
Collected in fees	Rs. 1,251-0-0

While the task of pioneering medical mission work in this needy village of Pusad has not always been easy, yet the satisfaction, experience, and results gained have made it very worth while. We have our daily clinics each morning, and the afternoons have been taken up in calls to the sick who are unable to come to the dispensary, and for other visitation work. We have always found the people very friendly and deeply grateful for the help they have received. Also we have had many opportunities of presenting the message of Jesus to them, and it has been pathetic so often to witness the deep hunger on the faces of the precious listening ones.

Here I would express my deep gratitude to God for His ever-abiding presence day by day. I don't think in all my life have I been so closely aware of the subtilty of the evil one and how he works, but the result is that Christ has become so infinitely precious. Praise His wonderful name! Jesus saves and sanctifies me now, and His promise still remains true: "Lo I am with you alway."

Ruth Freeman

In spite of interruptions and things to keep me in the house, we have still been able to carry on the village visitation work among Hindu and Mohammedan women. My only help, the pastor's wife, has a small child and is often unable to leave the home. Still we have managed to get into the village for calls quite often, sometimes as often as two or three times per week, sometimes less. Other times we have held meetings for the women in the waiting room of the dispensary. This always means acting quickly, grabbing up the opportunity while the women are all there in the waiting room. The singing of hymns often brings in other women from the street.

Again, at times, I have gone out alone to do visitation work in some little new neighborhood. And there are many of them, since Pusad has a population of some 15,-000. While I have been talking with these women in their homes, reading God's Word, and praying with them, God has abundantly blessed my own heart and has encouraged me in Him. Sometimes I have given them my own personal testimony. But more often it has been my habit to read to them from God's Word, and then tell them about Christ, the Saviour of the world. Each time I go away with great blessing on my own soul and a realization that this is certainly God's work and His way to get the message to these needy ones.

Earl G. Lee, Superintendent of the Bible School

There have been several factors that have led to a period of unusual success for the Bible school. Above all is the wonderful guidance and presence of God, and to Him be all the glory.

This year we have twelve couples and five single men. It will be of interest for you to know that the educational average among the men is the seventh standard. This goes to emphasize the fact that in Bible schools we are forced to take those who seem worthy irrespective of higher education and then do our best. We have found that some of the lesser educated men are proving to be good, hard-working students. There has been a very minimum of friction in the school and the co-operation among the students has been all that one could desire. We honestly feel that many of the students have really experienced entire sanctification and are growing in that grace.

Besides the regular work of the curriculum we have endeavored to carry on a rather heavy evangelistic program on the district. Week ends the boys have been divided into three groups and have gone to three different sections, concentrating in these places for the full school year. In one place fruit has already come, and we see evidence now that soon in the other places baptisms will be taking place. All told the boys have preached the gospel in seventy-eight different villages, many of which had never before heard the name of Jesus, and we must remember that all of this is within a twelve-mile radius of Basim. One thousand, two hundred and twenty Gospels have been sold.

Every student is trained in the Laubach system of teaching illiterates to read and write, and last summer they did fine work out in the villages. One of our students came back with a letter written by a government officer commending his work. His sense of service to his fellow Indians made a lasting impression on this officer. Again, this summer we hope to have the students work in Adult Literacy work.

I feel more than ever that I am in the center of God's will. I love the Lord with all my heart, I love the land to which I have been called and I love the people I serve. I have counted it a rare privilege to labor with my fellow missionaries and appreciate their work and fellowship. Best of all, the Lord is with us.

Hazel Lee

My days here in India remind me of a child's Christmas stocking, full, bulging, and overflowing, with something always sticking out on top that cannot be squeezed into the day no matter how hard I try. Since my coming to India God has taught me many valuable lessons. I have learned it is not the interruption that matters; it is the spirit in which I take it. It is not the size of my task that matters; it is doing every little thing as unto Him. It is not the denseness of the shadows of illness and sorrow that matters; it is keeping a whining "why" out of my prayers. A "disciplined prayer life" is a "must" on the mission field.

I have learned enough secrets of nursing to almost qualify for an R.N. degree. As I look at my chubby, healthy baby boy I can't help thinking of those hot days in a little Indian hospital where he lay like a wax doll fighting for his life. I did not pray for God to spare his life. I prayed for His will to be done and for grace to bear it. As his life nearly flickered out, God seemed to say to the angel of death, even as He did to Abraham, "Lay not thine hand upon the lad, neither do thou any thing unto him," and God gave him back to us. During Grant's convalescence I was severely tested physically. I felt so ill that I did not see how I could finish my term in India. No one but God knew the tremendous battle I fought. But one day I became conscious of a gradual change, a sense of strength being renewed until I realized that God had miraculously touched my body and I was able to pick up the reins of missionary work which had been slack for so long. I don't know how it happened; all I know is that prayers were answered and I was made whole. All praise be to our precious Lord!

In July Gary went away for his second year in boarding school. This separation becomes more difficult each time. I have an acute sense of being deprived of many wonderful privileges a mother should have. But God is watching over Gary. He is in a fine Christian school, finding an outlet for his boundless energy, doing well in his lessons, and receiving sound religious training. No, this does not spell "home and loved ones" to him now, but it will help to spell "adjustment" to him in the years to come. A lonely mission station is no place for an active little boy to become well-rounded. Every time he leaves me and always during his absence I feel like here is my one and only sacrifice on the mission field.

For this coming year I ask no easy way. All I ask is that, sunshine or shadow, valleys or hilltops, I shall ever be conscious of the form of the Fourth, the Son of God, who has trod the way before me and is now leading me in the way I should take. This is full, rich, abundant living. Life could hold no more!

Bronell A. Greer

We arrived back in Bombay on May 16, 1950. When the rains broke a month later, we proceeded to Basim, where we have since supervised the work of the Basim District and taught four classes in the Bible school: Ethics, Holiness, Practics, and Homiletics.

Outside of writing and publishing the Marathi *Preachers' Magazine,* and the preparation and printing of the *B.K.C.C. Prayer Diary,* the last four months have been spent almost entirely in evangelistic work among the non-Christians. We have preached 109 times and traveled over nine thousand miles.

For seven days in Mongrel Pier we had record attendance and attention. The next five days were filled with opposition from three sources. The first opposition party opened up a loud-speaker directed on our audience. We immediately closed our service and went over to their meeting. They invited me to sit with them as they spoke against me and Christianity. After several speakers, I was invited to speak. God helped me. A friendly spirit settled down upon us. The opposition leaders served us tea after the meeting, and the chief opposer came around the same evening for a personal apology. He has since come to Basim to pay us a visit. The next opposition was from students who later invited us to speak at their school. We did. The last opposition was from a young man who organized children to throw dust and stones at us in our service. The report is that the father of this man has now ordered his son to leave home, or apologize for his actions.

The Christ who dwells within has encouraged me to believe that the dawn of India's day, long prayed for and expected, is at hand.

Paula Greer

As we slowly pulled into Alexandria dock at Bombay as we returned from furlough, a deep calm settled over my soul, a calm which never leaves me in India no matter what the circumstances. I am sure it comes from perfect assurance of being in the center of God's will.

I was permitted to be on tour for about two months visiting the villages. During these times I often felt like the sower who went forth to sow. I could see that some of the seed was falling on the hard pathway and that Satan immediately snatched it away. There were times when there was wholehearted agreement among the women to our message, but the next day the interest had died away. The soil was shallow and the sun hot. Many times there seemed to be acceptance, but then the fruit was not realized because of the cares of life, of husband, of caste—all these crowded out the fruit. But then I am confident that some of the seed fell on fertile soil and that there will be a harvest of fruit. I can only pray that the Master of the Harvest will send the rain and sunshine in their seasons and reap to himself an abundance.

Evelyn M. Witthoff, M.D.

Because of being the only doctor on the field, I have had a very busy year. I praise God for His help and definitely touched me physically, and has kept me well strength, for without Him I could do nothing. He has in spite of strenuous work.

I have always been interested in the village clinics, so therefore I disliked to dispense with them when Dr. Speicher left on furlough. By not having a clinic at the hospital on Wednesdays I have been able to maintain these clinics, and to add a few more to them. Thus each month I have visited six villages. These clinics are growing, and we hope are helping to pave the way for the gospel in these places.

Besides the village clinics and the hospital work, there have been sick missionaries to care for from time to time. We have had the privilege to help not only our own missionaries but several from our neighboring missions. When my time has not been filled with medical duties it has been taken up with numerous details, such as the ordering of medicines and supplies, the paying of bills, caring for the animals, supervising whitewashing and repairs, and trying to catch up on the ever-present correspondence.

It seems each year the hospital is faced with some major problem, such as plague, or war. This year we have an acute water shortage, and may be forced to close the hospital earlier than usual because of it. We are praying that God will give us some good living water on our compound, for our future depends on it.

The following are the statistics from April, 1949, to April, 1950. During May and June the hospital was closed.

Total number of inpatients 617
Total number of outpatients 4,692
Number of deliveries 114
Number of operations 20
Services held (in addition to
    regular chapel) 50
Money collected from patients
    as fees .... Rs. 20,050-12-3 or $4,266

Money received on regular budget
.... Rs. 19,026-08 or $4,048
Money received as specials ....Rs. 2,636 or $560
(Mostly for duty and beds)

Geraldine Chappell

July 18, 1950, began my career in the Reynolds Memorial Hospital. Among my first experiences was the buying of nursing supplies in a village fifty miles from Basim. As the annex for sick and visiting missionaries is a part of the hospital progress, this soon became my responsibility.

Then, it wasn't long until I gave out the weekly boarding and hospital supplies. We were low on wheat and rice. I therefore had another buying trip.

On the afternoon of August 4, I launched out into the deep with my first Marathi class in "Nursing Ethics." Since then, I have also ventured into teaching "Dietetics."

And now there is the supervision of the hospital *shimpu* (tailor) and other hospital workers; the teaching of nurses; helping the W.F.M.S. women in making clothing for the Dhad school; incidental housekeeping; and the putting away of hospital parcels. You may say that this is not nursing, but it is a part of a nurse's life in India. Then come the days of relief for the doctor, the giving of intravenous injections and anaesthetics, and the delivery of babies.

Yes, I have learned—am still learning, I trust—to live more fully for Him. He saves and sanctifies me just now.

He said to me one day:
"I've called you to give
In such a forgetful way
That you My will shall live
In all your day.

"You are but clay in this land
For Me to melt, to mold in My hand.
If you will be molded, then, yield on, you must;
For great is the challenge, and averred is the trust."

I straightened my shoulders;
  I looked into His face,
And found what I needed,
  The overcoming grace.

Jean Darling

When I started to work in the hospital in 1946, I despaired at times as, day by day, there seemed to be little evidence or hope for progress as far as the nursing was concerned. But by July, 1949, the work was organized into four departments, with a graduate nurse—from our own first graduating class of that year—in charge of each department. The teaching of classes was difficult, for there were no Marathi textbooks available for the Mid-India area, and those of Bombay presidency were beyond my Marathi and beyond the needs of our hospital. So I tried to work out the courses practical for our needs and our nurses, and have them translated into Marathi. Now Miss Nalini Yangad is with us since last August and is teaching the student nurses three hours per day. Her help is most valuable, and this has meant one more step in the progress of the nursing school. With her as instructress, and Mrs. Bhagubai Nade in charge of the nurses, there are four full-time graduate staff nurses, as well as one part-time nurse, and eleven students, three of whom entered training August, 1950. This happens to be the exact ratio of staff nurses to student nurses, and students to number of hospital beds, as outlined by the Mid-India Board of Examiners. We have a long way to go yet; but this past year, as I have had the privilege of working with Dr. Witthoff and Miss Chappell, we have tried to raise the standard, not only in our nursing service, but in the standard of deeper Christian living, so that God can reach needy souls through us.

It is not the instrument in the hand of the surgeon, but the surgeon, who ministers to the patient; and so, in India, as an instrument, I have felt just as helpless, but just as confident, in the hand of my Saviour. If God has been able in some small way to use me for India, in a far greater measure through India He has ministered unto me. Today, for having lived and worked in India, I feel rich in my soul. So rich, for the privilege to be one of our missionary group, for each missionary has contributed much to my life; so rich, for the friends he has given among those to whom He calls me; so rich, for the promises given and for the prayers answered; so rich, when I look into my Saviour's face and know that I am in His will! Today, I am so rich!

Helen Rice
Ralph Rice
Mary Furnas